Redefining Matter Management:
A Best Practice Guide to Improving Processes and Profitability

EDITED BY HARRY LAWRENCE

Head of events and books
Leah Darbyshire

Commissioning editor
Alex Davies

Editorial assistant
Harry Lawrence

Published by ARK Group:

UK, Europe and Asia office
5th Floor
10 Whitechapel High Street,
London, E1 8QS
United Kingdom
Tel: +44(0) 207 566 5792
publishing@ark-group.com

North America office
4408 N. Rockwood Drive, Suite 150
Peoria IL 61614
United States
Tel: +1 (309) 495 2853
publishingna@ark-group.com

www.ark-group.com

Printed in the United Kingdom by Ashford Colour Press Limited, Gosport, Hampshire

ISBN: 978-1-78358-314-0

A catalogue record for this book is available from the British Library

ARK Group is a division of Wilmington plc. The company is registered in England & Wales with company number 2931372 GB. Registered office: 5th Floor, 10 Whitechapel High Street, London, E1 8QS.

VAT Number: GB 899 3725 51.

Contents

Executive summary

Time – as they say – is money. It is not an uncommon fact that lawyers today spend unnecessary amounts of time seeking out information, and therefore unnecessary amounts of money. In well-established fields, change is often slow; perhaps none more so than in the legal world. Though progress is being made, uptake has been rather slow, much to the dismay of those in the information management business.

Conversely to its cousin, case management, matter management should be thought of more in terms of low-volume but high-value information. The process thus lends itself nicely to forming centralized systems within organizations. It is so pervasive as to allow users to make decisions (e.g. conflict resolution) before matters are even opened, and can maintain a high level of time data accuracy and transparency via unalterable fundamental data.

From innovative and simple interfaces to enhanced reporting tools, from notification systems to customizable workflows, triumphs within matter management have enabled companies to become more efficient by saving time and money, and to engage stakeholders in a meaningful way. *Redefining Matter Management: A Best Practice Guide to Improving Processes and Profitability* is a collection of case studies that highlights some of the most important achievements and ideas in the field today. It is split into 10 chapters.

In Chapter 1, Aileen Leventon, principal at Edge International, outlines how law departments can effectively implement legal project management (LPM) as a tool for enhancing performance and adding value to their services. She describes the role of the legal department with reference to its inherent challenges, and breaks it down into five questions – why, what, when, how, and who. To round off, she runs through the four stages through which all legal matters flow – intake, planning, execution, and review – and outlines the various tools that can be leveraged to manage them.

Further building on the theme of LPM in Chapter 2, Barbara Boake, national practice leader at McCarthy Tetrault, and Rick Kathuria, national director, project management office and legal innovation at Gowling WLG, outline a framework that can help lawyers manage the two-fold responsibility of performing the legal work itself and managing the work within a budget. This framework divides a legal project into its component project parts (as opposed to its substantive legal parts) as follows: define, plan, monitor and evaluate.

Catherine MacDonagh, CEO and founder at the Legal Lean Sigma Institute, relates the foundational concepts of Lean Six Sigma to various approaches to matter management in Chapter 3. She touches on the application of Lean Six Sigma to loan services, and how process improvement can be integrated within project management, auditing and litigation. She uses real-world cases at various firms and interweaves them with the theory behind process improvement to form a clear picture of the opportunistic and systematic approaches to employing the methodology, and how to deliver greater value from them.

Chapter 4 looks at how elements of project management, Lean Six Sigma, and knowledge management (KM) can complement one another to drive a process improvement program. We see how Littler Mendleson approached challenges and opportunities to reengineer their case management processes, create a new approach and learn valuable insights along the way. Via the "define, measure, analyze, improve, control" (DMAIC) methodology, a core tool in Lean Six Sigma, Scott Rechtschaffen, the firm's chief knowledge officer, provides examples from law firms that have successfully employed both the full approach and the accelerated kaizen method to streamline their processes and boost profits.

Law firm KM succeeds when lawyers use it throughout their matters and when knowledge collection requires minimal extra work. However, matters are not static – they evolve through time. It is therefore necessary to focus on the entire matter lifecycle to genuinely understand and improve the underlying "assembly line" of processes. Chad Ergun, chief information officer at Davis Graham & Stubbs LLP, focuses on data-driven KM and matter lifecycle management in Chapter 5, and shows how they can be used as a means of combining past management experience and data analytics into an integrated decision-making approach that enables firms to be more competitive.

We see how the development of an innovation strategy is much more than a marketing device in Chapter 6 as Keith Lipman, progenitor of Matter Centricity and co-founder of Prosperoware, and Toby Brown, chief practice officer at Atkin Gump walk you step by step through matter taxonomy, matter types, matter sub-types and the matter task-coding process. They give a detailed explanation of how to use matter management to capture critical data and take knowledge management to a new, strategic level.

Director of strategic pricing and project management at Pepper Hamilton LLP, Peter Lane Secor, gives an overview of componentized pricing in Chapter 7. After a practical and succinct summary of componentized data, he discusses how to go about collecting it with reference to matter management and data collection systems in order to create a cost-benefit analysis, and how to implement that as a communication tool between firms and their clients. As clients start to scrutinize their legal spend more, Secor stresses, the importance of having a living document that details the exact cost and value of each activity and resource increases in line.

Chapter 8 has Sally Dyson, director at Firm Sense Limited guide us through the fundamentals needed to truly understand the cost of conducting matters, all the way from understanding why budgets are necessary, through showing how to create a matter budget, to tools that enable firms to execute them effectively.

Anthony Davis and Wendy Wen Yum Chang reflect on the concept of "bad revenue" in Chapter 9, and how firms are moving away from the "any work is profit" mentality to explore how they can use the client intake process to boost profitability. They bring to light the fact that, with proper client management and the confidence to reject those clients destined to be unprofitable, a firm can make significant improvements to its profits and explain how firms can take steps towards automating their client intake processes.

Finally, Peter Bennett, partnership executive officer, explains how Bates Wells Braithwaite implemented a matter level risk management system in Chapter 10 and, by assessing risk at matter level, saved the firm £6 million in insurance premiums. He makes the case for leveraging existing technology to improve operational risk management and making risk management part of the fee-earning process.

About the authors

Peter Bennett has been chief operating officer (COO) of Bates Wells Braithwaite (BWB) since 2006. During that time, BWB has expanded from £8 million to £25 million with a 225 headcount, converted to an LLP and then to an ABS, and has become the only law firm in the UK to gain world accreditation for being a socially responsible profit-making business (B Corps). Peter is the compliance officer for finance and administration (COFA), risk manager, data protection officer, he leads the risk and compliance service as well as having director level reports in accounting, human resources (HR), finance, and information technology (IT). A director of professional standards and risk will complete the management expansion in August 2016.

Peter is a member of the management board working closely with BWB's managing partner. He represents BWB on two expanding non-law joint ventures as well as the BWB CIO charity, and also serves as the honorary treasurer of a major charity. He has a total of 28 years of experience as chief officer in law firms. Three of these were solicitors, including BLM and two were barristers' chambers including Maitland Chambers.

Barbara J. Boake is the national practice leader and a partner within the bankruptcy and restructuring group at McCarthy Tétrault LLP in Toronto. Barbara has extensive experience in acquisitions, dispositions and restructurings of financially distressed corporations. She also advises US and Canadian high-yield investors in their debt-trading activities. She has been involved in the restructuring proceedings under the CCAA of US Steel Canada, one of Canada's largest integrated steel producers, and was administrator of Nortel's Canadian pension plans in Nortel's global restructuring proceedings. She also led the development and implementation of the firm's Dialogue Project Management® program and co-authored *Project Management for Lawyers*, published by Ark Group in 2011.

In 2009, Barbara was named one of the Top 100 Most Powerful Women in Canada by the Women's Executive Network (WXN). She is listed in the current editions of *Chambers Global: The World's Leading Lawyers for Business* and *Chambers Canada* as a leading lawyer in the area of restructuring and insolvency. She was also named one of the top 40 international restructuring professionals under 40 by the Global Insolvency and Restructuring Review. In addition to her legal experience, Barbara has acted as a senior advisor to the Minister of Finance (Ontario).

Barbara received her LLB from The University of Western Ontario in 1985. She was called to the Ontario bar in 1987.

Toby Brown is chief practice management officer at Perkins Coie LLP. He leads the firm's revenue management and efficiency programs, legal project management, pricing, process improvement, practice innovation, alternative staffing and new partner integration. Toby has more than a decade of experience in practice management and pricing with Am Law firms and is the former director of the Utah State Bar.

Toby is an active member and leader in organizations devoted to legal knowledge management, and he speaks to national audiences on legal pricing, alternative fee arrangements and other law firm financial management issues. He is the founder of the Legal Marketing Association's annual P3 Conference, which brings together more than 400 pricing, project management and process improvement experts in the legal profession. Toby also co-founded the "3 Geeks and a Law" blog and co-authored the book *Law Firm Pricing: Strategies, Roles and Responsibilities*.

Wendy Wen Yun Chang is a partner at Hinshaw & Culbertson LLP. She represents lawyers in all types of complex matters that involve the practice of law, including risk management counseling, ethics, crises management, outside general counsel support, disqualification motions, fee-related issues, discipline defense, hotline counseling, professional liability defense and ethics litigation. She is a certified specialist in legal malpractice law by the State Bar of California's Board of Legal Specialization, and is a member of the American Bar Association's Standing Committee on Ethics and Professional Responsibility. She also served as an advisor to the State Bar of California's Commission for the Revision of the Rules of Professional Conduct and is a past chair of the State Bar of California's Standing Committee on Professional Responsibility and Conduct.

Wendy also represents businesses in all types of business litigation, with particular emphasis on high exposure complex litigation, trials and appeals. She represents corporate and governmental entities in a variety of high-exposure media interest litigation, including complex tort defense, fraud and conspiracy claims, insurance litigation (coverage litigation, bad faith), contracts, and complex business disputes from filing through mediation, trial, arbitration, and/or appeal. She regularly appears before the trial courts and the courts of appeal. She represents businesses in defense of employment litigation, in discrimination, harassment and retaliation claims and has served as an independent workplace investigator for public entities in sensitive matters relating to human resource issues.

Anthony Davis is a partner at Hinshaw & Culbertson LLP. He is best described as a lawyer's lawyer. He is a member of the Lawyers for the Profession® practice group, and his practice focuses on the laws that govern lawyers. He advises attorneys and law firms on legal professional and ethics issues, law firm creation, merger and dissolution, risk management and loss control.

Sally Dyson is the founder and director of Firm Sense Limited, a consultancy specializing in providing client listening services and client relationship management advice to law firms. Sally qualified as a solicitor and practiced at Slaughter and May. She then worked as an in-house lawyer for nearly a decade before moving on from the pursuit of law to establish Firm Sense.

Sally combines expertise in client listening with an in-depth understanding of the legal market to advise law firms on aligning organizational practices and individual behavior with specific client needs in order to improve client retention, win business, and improve profitability. She is an Affiliate Member of, and is regulated by, the Market Research Society.

In the context of optimizing client relationships, she has developed particular knowledge on the topic of law firm fees and is the author of an Ark Group report entitled *Budgeting and Negotiating Fees with Clients: A Lawyer's Guide*. She is also a regular speaker at public conferences and private workshops and is a contributor to professional journals.

Chad Ergun has 20 years of experience in the legal technology sector, and has been driven by the idea that technology should be able to offer more to the business of running a law firm and its clients. Chad's focus has been in designing data-driven knowledge management platforms, improving practice services, offering advanced e-discovery solutions, and client-facing initiatives. Over the years, Chad has honed his expertise as he has worked to understand and build solutions across areas like knowledge management, practice support, business intelligence, e-discovery, finance, marketing, and human resources. In his current role, Chad leads the global practice services, business intelligence, and knowledge management groups at Gibson Dunn with members in multiple locations covering practice solutions, e-discovery, business intelligence, litigation support, application development, marketing technologies, knowledge management, and desktop and web applications. Chad holds a master's degree in information technology with a minor in industrial management and workplace psychology. He is currently working on his PhD in information management, focusing on artificial intelligence and data mining.

Bart Gabler is the director of pricing and legal project management for K&L Gates. In this role, Bart has global responsibilities to oversee the development of creative fee arrangements to meet client business objectives and develop tools to enable effective matter management and process improvement. He manages a team of professionals that drive analytical, matter management, and process improvement enhancements across the firm. Bart is a management team member who works collaboratively with cross-functional teams that includes K&L Gates lawyers on developing, negotiating and implementing strategic pricing arrangements and client budgets.

He also works directly with client service teams on pricing-related issues, including helping to identify client business objectives, cost pressures, and pricing preferences to ensure seamless client service. In addition, Bart is responsible for developing, implementing and coordinating the firmwide matter management platform, ensuring appropriate training of lawyers and professional staff to use these tools, and implementing best practices in matter management. He coordinates across K&L Gates' global platform of offices and practices to implement processes and tools to assist in matter planning and monitoring to help ensure effective and efficient client service.

With over 15 years of professional experience, Bart previously was a consultant with McKinsey & Company, where he served in both a client service and practice management capacity. His experience cuts across strategic planning and growth strategies to organizational transformation and effectiveness. He was also involved in the assessment of business requirements and staffing needs for project planning. Prior to McKinsey & Company, Bart was a strategy consultant with PricewaterhouseCoopers, where he conducted competitor analyses, evaluated operational strategies, and assessed current state business capabilities.

Rick Kathuria is national director, project management and legal logistics, at Gowling WLG. In this role, he leads the firm's business transformation agenda and legal project management strategy, applying process optimization and project management principles to the delivery of sophisticated legal services.

As a certified project management professional, certified management consultant and professional engineer (P.Eng.), Rick has over 15 years of experience working on large international projects at top-tier consulting firms. A noted authority on legal project management, he co-authored the book *Project Management for Lawyers* (Ark Group, 2011).

He is also a founding member and sat on the executive committee of the Project Management Institute's LPM initiative, promoting the education and adoption of LPM around the world. Rick is also a sessional professor at the University of Calgary's Law School where he teaches legal project management to the next generation of lawyers.

Aileen Leventon, JD, MBA, is a business counselor to the legal industry and a practicing lawyer with over 30 years of experience. She consults with law departments, law firms and individual lawyers on strategies to manage and sustain sound financial performance and continuously improve the efficiency of legal work. In addition to advising, coaching, and training, Aileen has facilitated numerous after-action reviews of closed matters to promote buy-in of legal project management techniques. She has also been embedded in ongoing matters to provide analysis and coaching to bring distressed matters back on course.

Keith Lipman is a well-regarded expert in the area of information management and e-discovery, in which he has been involved for almost two decades. Prior to founding Prosperoware, he was the director of legal solutions at iManage, Interwoven, and Autonomy iManage. He developed the go-to-market strategy for iManage in the legal industry and was the progenitor of matter-centric collaboration and the electronic file in WorkSite 8. Before iManage, Keith served in a number of professional capacities, including paralegal, lawyer, IT director in a law firm, and technology consultant to law firms.

Keith earned his BA, JD, and MBA at Temple University. He is a frequent speaker and is a contributing author of the book *Corporate Governance Best Practices: Strategies for Public, Private, and Not-for-Profit*

Organizations. He has also authored a number of articles on e-discovery and the management of email, documents, and records.

Catherine Alman Macdonagh, JD is a former corporate counsel and law firm executive. She now teaches and provides training and consulting services with a focus on process improvement, project management, operational and process excellence, organizational development and strategy.

A Legal Lean Sigma® Black Belt and a certified Six Sigma Green Belt, Catherine is the CEO and a Founder of the Legal Lean Sigma Institute, which offers consulting and the first and only process improvement and project management certifications, courses, and workshops designed specifically for the legal profession. Catherine developed Legal Lean Sigma® as well as the Legal WorkOut®, a collaborative method for lawyers, business professionals, and clients to engage in process improvement together that has won multiple awards, including the 2018 Process Excellence Award for Best Business Transformation Process at the OPEX Week: Business Transformation World Summit.

Catherine is an adjunct professor at Suffolk Law School and George Washington University (Master's in Law Firm Management) and a frequent guest lecturer at other academic institutions. She is the author of *Lean Six Sigma for Law Firms* and the co-author of *The Woman Lawyer's Rainmaking Game* and *The Law Firm Associate's Guide to Personal Marketing and Selling Skills.* She is a contributing author to six books: *Redefining Matter Management: A Best Practice Guide to Improving Processes and Profitability; The Lawyer's Guide to Project Management; The Bigger Picture: Driving Client Value Through Collaboration; The Lawyer's Guide to Process Improvement;* and *The Procurement Handbook.*

Scott Rechtschaffen is chief knowledge officer at Littler Mendelson and leads Littler's effort to provide innovative client services by integrating new technologies and work processes and enabling attorneys and clients to access the collective knowledge and experience of the firm's more than 1,000 attorneys. He combines over 25 years of experience representing companies in every area of labor and employment law with a broad understanding of technology to help the firm's attorneys and their clients in tailoring unique solutions that enhance the firm's ability to deliver legal information and legal services to its clients. Scott heads Littler's knowledge management department, comprising of dedicated KM attorneys, research specialists, and technologists. He was a member of the multi-disciplinary team that developed the award-winning Littler

CaseSmart® approach to legal case management. He oversees the firm's electronic and print publications, internal KM systems, and online client subscription services. He is also the co-founder of ComplianceHR, an innovative joint venture launched by Littler and Neota Logic, a legal software company.

Scott has been awarded the Distinguished Peer Award as KM Champion of the Year by the International Legal Technology Association, named to the Fastcase 50 – an annual compilation "honoring the law's smartest, most courageous innovators" – and was named among the 10 most innovative lawyers in North America by the *Financial Times* in 2014.

Peter Lane Secor is the director of strategic pricing and project management with Pepper Hamilton LLP. He concentrates on legal project management with a focus on improving efficiencies through shared management responsibilities, strengthening communication, and making value transparent. Peter's expertise includes client/matter profit analysis and providing partners with performance evaluations from a financial perspective.

Chapter 1:
How law departments can use legal project management to enhance performance and add value

By Aileen Leventon, principal, North America, Edge International[1]

The discipline of project management provides a solid foundation for every activity conducted by a business. Legal project management (LPM) provides the discipline that enables law departments to define, demonstrate, and deliver greater value to their organizations by balancing the scope of work, time, and resources allocated to legal work more efficiently. Although some perceive LPM as complex, it is in fact what lawyers already do, only more systematically and using the language of business. At its core, effective project management is about sound communication at critical points with the right stakeholders.[2]

The threshold – Defining the role of the legal department

While each department may formulate its role differently, the fundamental challenge of lawyers in a business setting is to help clients achieve business goals, take advantage of opportunities, and protect against legal risk. Compliance with laws, regulations, and corporate policy are about both risk and reputation, which are integral to a company's business and culture.

Highly-regarded and effective in-house lawyers are known for certain behaviors, in addition to their substantive legal expertise. They demonstrate skills that reflect the role of a lawyer as a trusted advisor insofar as they:

- Understand all aspects of a client's business so legal services are calibrated to achieve the business definition of a successful result;
- Recognize that legal issues are one of many components in a client's business project or goal;
- Seek to add the most value by finding the lawyers with the appropriate level of experience who can support the business endeavor at the right time;

- Ensure that legal services and expenses and resources are aligned with business goals and strategies; and
- Participate in communication channels to ensure that the right level of communication occurs at the right time with the right stakeholders and professionals.

The general counsel and members of the legal department – lawyers, paralegals and operations professionals – are well-positioned to address these issues. They are able to integrate their understanding of the business context into everything they do, regardless of whether external counsel or other service providers are involved. In-house counsel manages the delivery of legal services to the client, while tactically managing a cost-effective action plan that achieves the client's business goals. LPM provides the tools and the methodology for meeting this challenge, while guarding against the impulse to work on the interesting legal issues at the expense of adding value to the company.

Representatives of the legal department also must translate the client perspective when retaining a law firm or other third party to participate in handling the matter. It is incumbent on the client to clearly articulate his or her view in order to guide the handling of the matter. How many discussions about the reasonableness of fees relate to the gap between outstanding legal work and the business needs of the client? And if the business needs are not well understood, to what extent is the inside counsel responsible for the lack of alignment? The law department must ensure that the entire legal team, including law firms, understand the importance of how the work is done, consistent with the corporate culture and needs.

Five questions to maintain focus

An LPM framework calls for legal team members to be able to answer five key questions at the launch of a matter and throughout its course in a manner appropriate to their roles.[3] The questions should be reconsidered at critical junctures, particularly because of the likelihood of changes in circumstances. As new information emerges, assumptions made at the outset may not hold. Stakeholders within the company may be problematic because of disparate definitions of a successful outcome. Even in the absence of change, as time goes on and as the composition of the team evolves, it is important to confirm that all are headed toward the same goal in a consistent manner.

The five questions relate to both process (how the work is done) and substantive legal strategy and tactics:

1. *Why* we are handling this matter for the business – why is it important to the company's strategy and operations?
2. *What* legal strategy will accomplish the business goal and what legal work is out of scope?
3. *When* and in what sequence must work be done and what are the uncertainties and dependencies regarding timing?
4. *How* do we manage the work, given constraints and requirements such as budget, strategic importance, regulatory and reporting obligations, timing, and risk management protocols?
5. *Who* is involved in the work and what is each person's role and responsibility?

The answers to these questions have consequences – positive, negative and neutral – for resource allocation, work plans, scope of work, stakeholders, roles and responsibilities, teamwork, training, communications throughout the project, status reporting and client satisfaction. The systematic analysis of these issues addresses the operational challenges of the legal department by reducing non-value added (or wasted) time, minimizing surprising outcomes and costs, managing overall costs and spending, and controlling time to completion more precisely.

Four stages of a matter

LPM applies the business discipline of project management across four stages through which all matters flow:

1. Intake;
2. Planning;
3. Execution; and
4. Review.

This framework, developed by a 2017 Corporate Legal Operations Consortium (CLOC) group of experts,[4] is illustrated in the chart below.

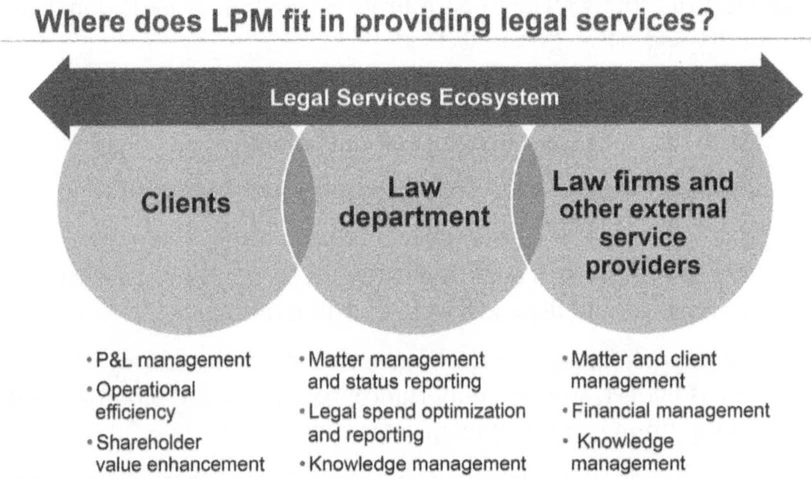

Figure 1: The CLOC Legal Project Management Framework for Legal Teams

Source: https://cloc.org/industry-guidelines – *CLOC Legal Project Management for Legal Teams; The Business Case and Action Plan for Legal Departments*

Intake

Intake occurs when the legal department becomes involved – after confirming the validity of the request as appropriate. A primary lawyer is assigned along with others in the department. At this stage, the legal team, in collaboration with the client and other stakeholders, should reach agreement on the goals, objectives and scope of the matter. Time constraints should be specified (e.g. close the deal by the end of the fiscal year; settle the case before there is a change in business unit management). The business and legal risks should be assessed along with the complexity of the matter.

At this point, in-house counsel determines appropriate resources with a "make vs buy" decision: should work be completed exclusively in-house or should outside counsel be engaged? If outside counsel is appropriate, it is essential to identify their role and the nature of the legal department relationship: is it collaboration, management, or outsourcing? Is there a "go-to" firm or is there a panel of options available if the matter is put out to bid? What fee structures are appropriate if financial agreements are not already in place? Consideration of these issues will lead to well-informed decision-making.

Planning

Planning does not just happen on its own. Effective lawyers start the planning process to ensure that the scope of the work is well-defined. This is the baseline for managing client expectations and guiding the work of the legal team. Clients express dissatisfaction when there is a gap between their needs and the lawyer's perception of her role. Team members are frustrated when work is inefficient, duplicative, or incomplete. A Statement of Work should be developed, with sign-off by the business client. The frequency of status checks, communication, and metrics for monitoring the matter should be determined early on. If outside counsel is to be involved, the retention and pricing arrangements need to be established in the initial planning stage. Development of a baseline plan and honest discussion at this stage is key to avoiding misunderstandings and tension as the matter unfolds.

While there are often too many meetings, the kick-off meeting is indispensable.[5] As the forum for collaborative planning, it sets the tone for sound stewardship of resources, accountability of team members, and goals of sound economics and delivery of value. Rapid action and deliberative planning can co-exist even though lawyers typically seek to act and adjust, rather than plan and execute.

Several LPM tools are useful at this stage to guide the discussion and confirm the scope of work. They include the project charter, the stakeholder analysis, and the work plan. Now is the time to discuss allocation of roles and responsibilities. A useful tool is a LACI/RACI chart.[6] All of these tools are discussed in more detail below. If outside counsel is involved, a budget should be formulated as the work plan is developed. It is critical to document the assumptions associated with the phases of work since they will be revisited as the matter evolves. It is also helpful to create a timeline or Gantt chart to reflect time constraints and the expected duration of phases of the matter. They too will be changed as the matter evolves, but having the estimate helps frame everyone's expectations about when they will need to be available. The work plan, Gantt chart, and the LACI chart are tools that communicate the sequencing of events that affect clients and members of the legal team. When used effectively, bottlenecks and fire drills are significantly reduced – even eliminated. The discipline of planning by using relevant tools helps overcome the chaos of "Ready, Fire, Aim!" that so many lawyers and clients have experienced.

Execution

Execution is the meat of handling the matter. In addition to the substantive legal work and engagement of the business client, there is also the need to continuously check that the work on the matter is meeting expectations.

1. Scope: Is the work being handled so that the scope that was established at the outset is on track? What needs to be managed to resist changes that do not meet the client's definition of success? Should anything else be monitored?
2. Scope creep: Is the work expanding for the legal team? Scope creep occurs when lawyers are asked to play a role that the client or a third party was expected to perform, circumstances change (facts, people, or the law), assumptions made at the outset are unfounded, or unanticipated events occur. Does outside counsel have more work to do than reflected in the statement of work or work plan? Are their legal fee expectations still appropriate?
3. Resource management: Is the legal team contributing an unexpected level of effort? Although one reason may be scope creep, there also may be turnover in members of the legal team or stakeholders who require education and transition time.
4. Costs: If third parties, such as outside counsel, e-discovery vendors, or contract lawyers are involved, how do fees and expenses compare to the budget? Variances need to be understood in detail, rather than characterized as overruns or poor budgeting. The timetable may have shifted with costs occurring earlier or later than expected. Assumptions and the occurrence of 'unknown unknowns' should be evaluated in reviewing a budget, forecast, and invoice.
5. Outcomes: Are the results meeting business and legal objectives for the matter as it evolves? The definition of success may change so it is important to determine if the plan still meets current goals. For example, an M&A deal that was strategic when launched because the company was entering a new market may be a bolt-on acquisition because another deal closed earlier; a litigation that is critical to a core business may become less significant because the business has been sold. The law governing the matter may have changed. The level of risk and effort varies based on the business and legal context, which needs to be confirmed with the client throughout the matter.

A well-managed matter is not a series of ad hoc reviews and scrambles to submit reports to management. It is an ongoing process that is embedded in regular and appropriate communication.

Review

Review is a stage that is often scuttled. It is all too easy to move on to the next matter and avoid any perception of failure. Nevertheless, the review stage is an excellent opportunity for legal teams to demonstrate the value of the legal department and their commitment to continuous improvement. In this stage, the client, in-house lead, and outside counsel should evaluate the results, particularly how the matter was planned, managed, and executed. Insights gathered during this stage ultimately lead to more successful outcomes and more efficient handling of similar work in the future.

During this stage, it is important to look for what worked well and should be replicated as a best practice. "Good work" should enhance future work – by engendering improved action plans, training opportunities, and templates. Watch the tendency to be hypercritical; find the positive. Remember that common practice is not the same as "best practice". Strive to raise the bar.

Identify the source of any tension that emerged among team members or with the internal client. Fertile areas for review are moments when things seemed to go off track, when progress was marred by misunderstandings, duplicative work, and surprises. Focus on the root cause of variances from plan and the steps taken to recover. Shifting stakeholders may have materially changed the scope of work and strategy. Concerns about business reputation or relationships with suppliers and customers may have caused a dramatic change in plans. Matters that at one point were mission-critical may have diminished in importance.

The review stage is the opportunity to determine what factors fostered or detracted from efficiency and the client's view of value. Soliciting the client's feedback demonstrates the legal team's commitment to achieving client satisfaction and following best practice. At this stage, it is important to identify the root cause of problems which led to legal department involvement. This not only prevents legal problems from arising in the future; it also opens the door for the legal team to be proactive with its client.

Pick the right tool

There are a number of project management tools that lawyers find are helpful. Start with the ones that seem the most useful. As a tool becomes integral to matter management, consider adding others to the toolkit:

- The project charter/statement of work – the statement of the goals and business case for the project, the work that is in and out of scope, the resources to be allocated to the project, and the point at which the project would be "done".
  - Misunderstandings here often set the team on the wrong course. For example, the business goals may not be clear or the strategy is inconsistent with the risk the project is addressing.
  - The project charter should be revisited as a matter progresses. Goals and the business case may change and require adjustments to the initial plan and strategy.
- Stakeholder analysis – identification of the internal people and business units and the external constituents who have a stake in or could affect the outcome and course of the project. Key stakeholders often are overlooked at the outset. The board of directors, the press and regulators are stakeholders, as are the head of a business unit, the CFO, and the lawyer in charge of the matter.
  - As additional stakeholders surface, the entire understanding of goals and strategies may change.
  - Conflicts may exist between various stakeholders that, if not addressed at the launch, may be a source of tension later on. A means for resolving differences among stakeholders, particularly among functions within an organization, should be established as part of the overall approach to communication.
- Assumptions – perceptions about the probable scope and course of the work from both a substantive and managerial perspective, a material change which could affect stakeholders, timing, work to be performed and/or the resources required to reach completion.
  - Experience allows the leaders of the legal team to make reasonable assumptions about a deal structure, a judge, an adversary, the due diligence process, the actions of third parties, etc., and to chart a project plan based on assumptions. Typically, this means decisions about what work will and will not be done.

  - Problems arise when assumptions are made in silence and circumstances change. If "no surprises" is the client mandate, assumptions must be explicitly discussed and often documented. The LPM framework requires the lawyers and clients to identify and communicate about assumptions.

- Work plan/time line – delineation of the phases of work, specific tasks, deliverables, decision points, time frame and sequencing of events. When the team embraces a good work plan, there is less rework, non-productive work, and disruptive activities.[7]
- LACI chart – a tool that formalizes the understanding – frequently unarticulated – about which specific individuals will lead or assist in the work and who should be consulted or informed about the progress of the matter. The LACI discussion provides clarity by reducing the likelihood of duplicative or unnecessary work, and ensures that someone is leading each component of the work.
- Communications plan – clear identification of who needs to be informed and consulted about status and any material changes. The communications plan involves:
  - Defining and managing the scope of the work;
  - Making sure all those who need to be involved are in the loop;
  - Making sure that risks are addressed on time by the right people;
  - Providing status updates;
  - Facilitating meetings and discussions; and
  - Communicating meeting minutes and action items to assure the matter stays on track.
- Budget by phase – the estimate and actual amount of resources allocated to each phase of the work. A more granular look at tasks at this point may divert attention from more essential issues.
- Review checklist – a sign-off from the client that there are no open items, which occurs within 45 days of the close of a matter. The list should include any management tools maintained by the law department or its outside counsel, and is an important way of determining what did or did not work and why. Are these findings specific to the matter or can they be utilized in other projects?

Metrics

No discussion on LPM is complete without mentioning how to measure its impact. In the business case and action plan[8] for LPM developed by a CLOC working group in 2017, the following chart shows where relevant metrics can be developed:

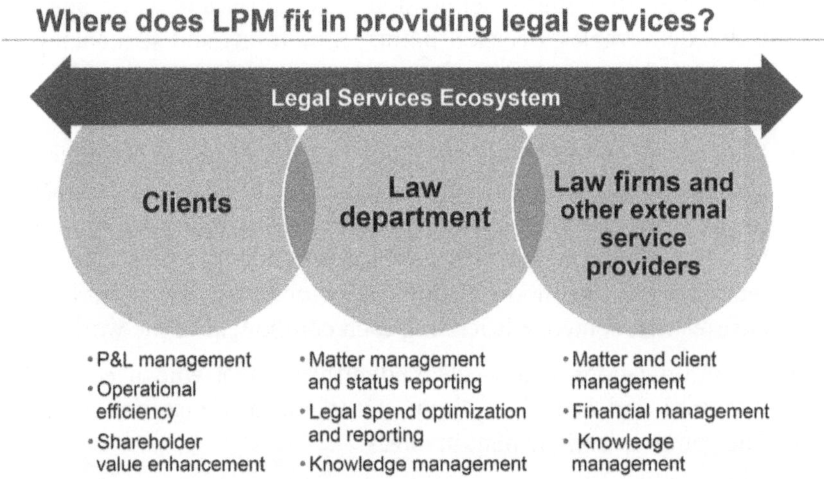

Figure 2: CLOC LPM business case and action plan

Source: https://cloc.org/industry-guidelines – *CLOC Legal Project Management for Legal Teams; The Business Case and Action Plan for Legal Departments*

Clients and the general counsel focus on managing the bottom line and enhancing shareholder value. The corporate profit and loss statement is affected by the cost of legal services, measured by aggregating the compensation and benefits of members of the legal department, allocated corporate overhead, spending on outside counsel and other third parties, and out of pocket expenses. Shareholder value is enhanced by transactions and resolution of litigation that affect the corporate balance sheet. Matter management, legal spend optimization and knowledge management are derivatives of these corporate goals.

The well-managed legal department keeps its eyes on metrics that indicate the extent to which these practices are achieved. The law firm, when involved, addresses its own economic goals.

A legal department seeking to develop metrics should consider the results of LPM and which aspects are worth measuring, as highlighted in the figure below.

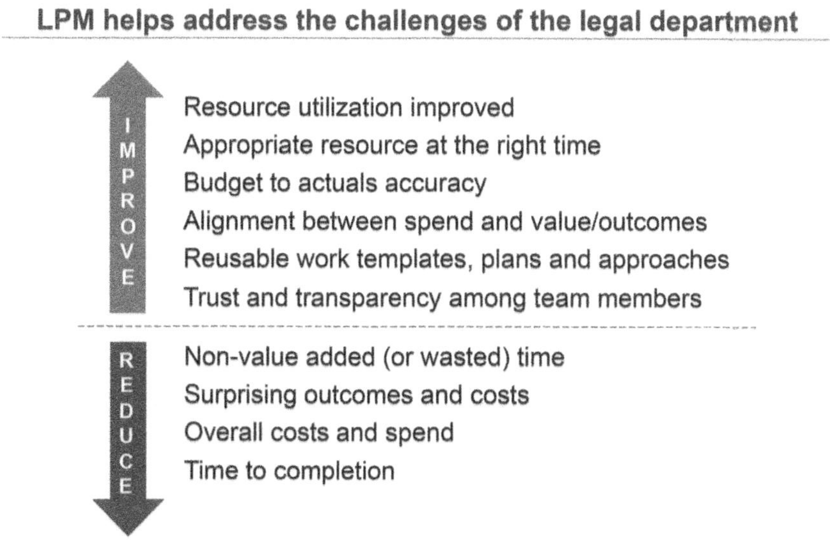

Figure 3: The benefits of LPM

Source: https://cloc.org/industry-guidelines – *CLOC Legal Project Management for Legal Teams; The Business Case and Action Plan for Legal Departments*

Conclusion

The role of lawyers in the corporate setting is to respond to a client's need for legal support in maximizing shareholder value and supporting corporate stewardship. Often the lawyer must guide the client to articulate the full range of business objectives and stakeholders in a situation. She evolves from the role of technical specialist and risk manager to a key participant in addressing business challenges and opportunities.

In-house counsel is uniquely situated to meld legal strategy and tactics with operational constraints that the business imposes. For most companies, this necessitates disciplined management of costs as well as the protection of its assets. Concurrently, counsel must model the behaviors that the client expects of other members of the business team: stewarding the client's resources and demonstrating accountability not only for what is done, but also for how it is done. In-house counsel manages the delivery of legal services to the client by focusing on a cost-effective action plan that achieves the client's business goals.

The timely delivery of information is the life-blood of a legal matter and a formal communication plan is its circulatory system. At its core, LPM is about effective communication, which enables the legal team to demonstrate its value.

References

1. This chapter reflects many years of collaboration with the author's former colleagues at QLex Consulting Inc., James Buckley and Nancy Lasersohn. Jim is the pioneer of LPM through his work as Associate General Counsel, Environmental Health and Safety at LockheedMartin Corporation as described in the three-part series 'Welcome to Lawyerland' in the ACC Docket (January–March 2005). After leaving Lockheed, he joined Nancy and me at QLex, where we introduced LPM to the DuPont Legal Department in 2011 under Thomas Sager's leadership as General Counsel. Tom has continued as an LPM proponent as a partner at Ballard Spahr LLP.
   The chapter heavily references a working group that has developed a LPM business case and resource for Corporate Legal Operations Consortium (CLOC) under the leadership of Connie Brenton, Patrick Ellis, and Pratik Patel. The Business Case and Action Plan and accompanying resources benefitted from all the participants in the initiative. Special thanks go to Janelle Belling (Perkins Coie LLP), Kevin Bielawski (Husch Blackwell LLP), Danny Kotlowitz (Telstra), Patrick Ellis (GM), Dan Safran (Legal Shift), and David Rueff, Jr (Baker Donelson) for their particular insights.
2. www.law360.com/articles/537101, Law Practice is Evolving Via 'Legal Project Management' (May 15, 2014); wwww.aileenleventon.com/publications
3. There are many frameworks, and they all support the same goal of managing the scope of work, planning and monitoring, and communication. Two examples that were developed for law firms are highlighted in S. Lambreth, A. Leventon, and D. Rueff, *Implementing Legal Project Management* (Createspace 2016). This book contains a detailed description of all the tools discussed in this chapter.
4. See https://cloc.org/industry-guidelines and to CLOC Legal Project Management for Legal Teams. See also www.aileenleventon.com/services.
5. See www.edge.ai/2017/04/one-meeting-you-must-have/
6. See Kleinman and Leventon, *Better-Faster-Cheaper Through Legal Project Management: The LACI Chart*, BNA Bloomberg, 2016.
7. When the phases and tasks of work are written down and shared among team members, the work plan becomes a communication tool for determining items that have been omitted (inadvertent or oversights) or are duplicative or inefficient. A fuller explanation, with examples, may be found at www.smartsheet.com/top-excel-project-plan-templates.
8. See Note 4, above.

Chapter 2: A simple legal project management framework

By Barbara J. Boake, national practice leader partner, McCarthy Tétrault LLP, and Rick Kathuria, national director of project management and legal logistics, Gowling WLG

Legal mandates are projects

In order to enhance the chances of a successful outcome, legal mandates should be managed as projects. Lawyers who lead significant matters must accept the dual responsibility of:

- Performing the legal work; and
- Managing the project.

These are two distinct roles. Lawyers have historically been experts in performing only the first role. A legal project management (LPM) framework provides a context within which lawyers can perform their less familiar role as project managers.

The framework divides a legal matter into its component project parts, which are distinct from its substantive legal or procedural parts. In this framework, these are referred to as project stages, project tasks and project deliverables, in order to distinguish them from the substantive stages, tasks and deliverables of a transaction or case.

Legal mandates have four project stages

Every legal matter can be broken down into four project stages:

- Define;
- Plan;
- Monitor; and
- Evaluate.

The project manager is responsible for moving the matter through each stage.

Figure 1 illustrates the four stages of a legal project life cycle. The five project management processes are depicted around the perimeter.

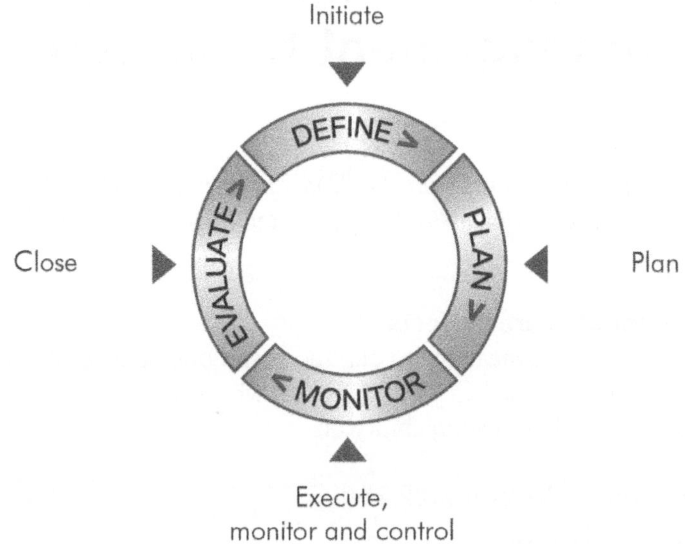

Figure 1: Legal project life cycle

This legal project life cycle departs from strict project management theory in a number of ways. The 'execution' and 'monitor/control' processes have been combined into one project stage. Although these are quite separate functions that are often performed by different individuals, they co-exist over the same period in a legal matter. In addition, the execution of legal work is second nature to lawyers and not something that requires highlighting as a distinct stage in a legal project management model.

The project stages are named with a view to emphasizing those elements of project management about which lawyers, in particular, need reminding – 'Define'; 'Plan'; 'Monitor'; and 'Evaluate'.

Each project stage has two project management tasks and one project management deliverable

In order to move a legal matter through each of the four stages, a project manager must ensure that the two tasks and one deliverable that are required at each stage are completed. These tasks and deliverables are depicted in Figure 2.

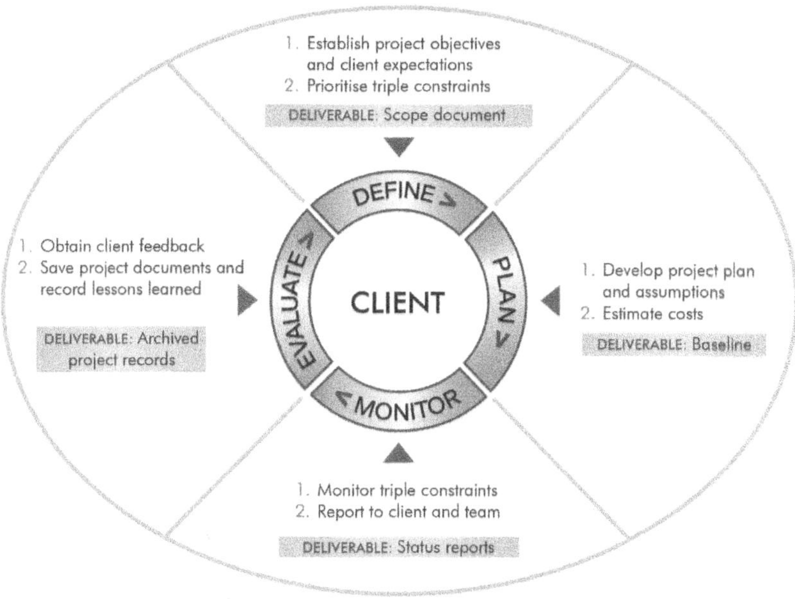

Figure 2: The LPM framework

Your client participates at every stage of the project

One of the purposes of adopting an LPM model is to provide law firms with the tools they need to give clients greater control over the cost and other outcomes of their legal matters. Consequently, before a project can move from one stage to the next, the client must agree with the project manager that the tasks and deliverables required at each preceding stage have been successfully completed. This requires continuous and effective communication between the project manager and client at every stage. Accordingly, the client is placed in the center of the LPM model as shown in Figure 2.

A project manager's responsibilities can be delegated

The lead lawyer on a matter will often delegate many of his/her responsibilities to another member of the team to perform or supervise the legal work. This is encouraged for project management responsibilities as well. However, given the importance of defining clear and achievable project objectives, it is recommended that the lead lawyer perform the tasks required in the first stage of a project. All other project management tasks and deliverables can be delegated to a more junior lawyer, a non-lawyer support individual or an administrative assistant, as appropriate.

Although delegation is encouraged, the lead lawyer must remain accountable to the client organization for the legal work product and to the sponsoring individual within that organization for the management of the project.

Designing a framework that works

Every law firm and legal department has its own unique culture and work style. The LPM model provided in this chapter was designed with the benefit of extensive trial and error, and uses tools and techniques that we believe are most relevant and useful in the practice of law. Although it should give you a head start, it will likely need to be refined or modified to work within your own organization.

Instituting project management in a law firm is not a quick fix. It is a challenge to the *status quo* that requires lawyers to change the way they have traditionally worked. Resistance is inevitable and the importance of strong and consistent leadership of the initiative should not be underestimated. In Chapter 10, we provide practical advice on how to develop and implement a LPM program in a law firm environment.

The business case for must be made and understood by the most senior levels of firm management before any work begins. As with any internal firm initiative, support from the firm leader will be critical to its success. The development of project management must be – and must be seen to be – one of your organization's highest priorities.

Careful consideration should be given to who will lead the initiative or, to use project management terminology, who will be the project 'sponsor'. This individual will set the objectives, timeline and budget and will have important decisions to make at every stage of the process. Accordingly, he/she should have direct access to executive authority. The project sponsor should also be someone who is well versed in firm culture and in the organization's ability to embrace change.

You will need a project manager. Internal law firm projects involving significant non-billable commitments can be extremely difficult to manage and sustain. It will be important to choose a project manager who is able to set reasonable expectations and find ways to keep the project moving forward.

Finally, and most importantly, the project sponsor and project manager must firmly believe in the value of project management and be able to withstand the inevitable resistance they will encounter, so that the project can be kept on track.

Chapter 3: Opportunistic approaches to employing Lean Six Sigma

By Catherine Alman MacDonagh, CEO and founder, Legal Lean Sigma Institute

While a systematic approach might be the most impactful, and the long term results it can produce the most desirable, the reality is that most firms begin by employing Lean Six Sigma opportunistically, taking advantage of pockets of interest and improving skills and discrete processes. This results in opportunistic improvements that are valuable but uneven across the organization and not always flowing to the bottom line.

Typically, opportunistic approaches occur because one person, usually a leader in a particular practice area or business function, determines that process improvement is worth trying. The most effective approach, in our experience, came from Morgan Lewis' e-data Group, which recently invited clients to a two-day course and earned Yellow Belt certifications by learning, and working on, the processes of greatest interest to them.

With ever more legal services being deemed "commodity" type work, and the use of fixed fees and value-based billing increasing, we know that there is increasing pressure for firms to be highly efficient. Even with an opportunistic approach, the chances for differentiation and developing signature approaches are significant – and firms that are using process improvement to seize these opportunities are reaping the rewards.

Morgan Lewis applies Six Sigma to loan services – since 1974

Applying process improvement to a specific service that is viewed as commodity work is not new. Morgan Lewis, for example, was at the forefront with Six Sigma in application to its mortgage loan services. According to a case study by Richard J. Sabat, Six Sigma Green Belt at Morgan Lewis, the firm began applying Six Sigma to its loan services starting in 1974. This was first employed institutionally in 1988 with FDIC/RTC, retooled in 1997 with Total Quality Management, and then again with Six Sigma in 2000/2003. This is one of the earliest and most specific case studies I could find when I began to build the first of the Legal Lean Sigma Institute's programs and certification courses (and then again in researching for and writing this chapter).

Sabat's case study provides excellent data on the approach used and the results achieved, including the fact that the firm was able to realize up to a 25 percent reduction in time charges and dramatically enhanced quality in mortgage loan services. While this type of reduction might not have been the most desirable result for a firm charging by the hour, it certainly is appealing to any client who is looking for the best, lowest cost solution, and to any firm performing the work for a fixed or capped fee.

Causes of defects (which is considered waste in Lean terms) were identified as: transaction data input, intermittent data flow, inefficient data communication to entire team, no data quality control, lack of standard forms, and poor-quality forms (the precedent documents contained defects and there was a lack of baseline and/or quality control). Additionally, the Socratic associate training method employed by the firm reportedly resulted in a lack of written transaction practices and written standard operating procedures. Finally, time pressure and disorganization were also identified as causes.

Using the data gathered in measure phase of the DMAIC framework, and the work performed in analyze phase, Morgan Lewis developed their improvement ideas, which included human behavior items such as client protocols and standard practices and procedures. They also focused on what Sabat refers to as the "physics of the transaction", meaning data input and integrity, standard forms, and standard communication. Interestingly, document preparation software was part of their solution.

The charts included in the case study show very compelling "before", "early Six Sigma", and "later Six Sigma" graphical results, indicating that the firm did not just improve the process once; they committed to continuous improvement and realized better results each time they improved how they performed and delivered work in this area.

Combining process improvement and project management at Fisher Matthews PLLC

One of the best examples of a service that realized extraordinary benefits from combining process improvement and project management comes from commercial real estate attorney Rebekah Fisher. Fisher, currently of Fisher Matthews PLLC, formerly of Waller Lansden Dortch and Davis, Dinsmore & Shohl LLP, developed an excellent process to prepare, negotiate, and execute a great number of commercial leases each year for a large retailer client. She improved her commercial real estate practice in a way that resulted in the highest levels of client satisfaction and excellent profitability for her practice and firm.

In order to perform this work profitably using an alternative fee structure for the portfolio of work, Fisher focused on standardizing her process, communications, forms, and leases. She explained that she uses only very organized and efficient timekeepers, which involves staffing with the lowest-cost resources capable of doing each activity. Detailed data about the effort it takes to both do and deliver this work is kept, which allowed Fisher to continually refine her model process and very effectively manage the work and resources.

The results are impressive. Fisher reports that they improved their response time from the receipt of the client's request to producing a draft of lease to either the same or the next day. They also reduced the overall time it takes from their receipt of the client's request to the execution of a lease from 168 days to 62 days.

It is important to translate improvements into benefits: Fisher's fast, reliable results have allowed the client to open stores an average of eight weeks earlier that was previously possible. This is worth tens of millions of dollars in increased revenue for their client. Thus, in addition to the fact that this process allows the law firm to deliver this service profitably and reliably for a low fixed fee, their client's high satisfaction with the results has them singing Fisher's praises. This, in turn, has resulted in new, referred business for the firm.

OFCCP audit process improvement at Ogletree, Deakins, Nash, Smoak & Stewart, P.C

An improved OFCCP audit process was one of the many projects tackled at Ogletree, Deakins, Nash, Smoak & Stewart, P.C. This project was championed by practice group leader Leigh Nason, whose practice includes representing federal contractors and sub- contractors in compliance evaluations and administrative enforcement actions triggered by the United States Department of Labor's Office of Federal Contract Compliance Programs (OFCCP).

The project team included lawyers, paralegals, knowledge management professionals, and data analysts. The goals of the project were to create a consistent, branded process for AAP preparation,

OFCCP audit defense, and various other services such as EEO-1 reporting, compliance assessments, etc. – anything in the group's area of service that would benefit from a consistent workflow process, define the lowest cost timekeeper capable of doing a task and ensure that appropriate work is funneled to those people, promote the new process internally (to their referrers) and externally (to new and existing clients), and ensure that all practice group members are "on board" with the new process.

Additionally, Nason wanted to train and generate awareness among other practice group members and referrers within the firm as to what the service was and how the work was performed. Furthermore, she knew that it was important to "ensure a basic level of competence among all attorneys and specialized knowledge of various areas (such as applicant/hire analysis, testing, etc.) among a few attorneys. The improved process had to facilitate the ability to generate a specific dollar amount (number intentionally omitted) in additional revenue and we had to be able to measure that revenue with some degree of certainty."

Moreover, the project goals included an increase in practice group services- related billings of each timekeeper (other than the top generator) by at least 10 percent. Underlying this idea was the need to create such a good process that Nason, the practice group leader, could manage a "virtual" practice group of attorneys, analysts, and staff in various offices.

After measuring and analyzing many aspects of the process, the team drew inspiration from great coaches and sports teams to develop creative improvements and solutions. Examples included developing a "playbook" with a current roster/directory, and specific "plays" (checklists, forms, etc.) so that quality assurance and consistency is guaranteed, regardless of the client or attorney working on the project. The team also clarified guidelines regarding credits, opening matters, and rates and also ensured that the premium rates for this niche practice work were not "watered down" by insurance rates.

As is the case with many (even most, if not all) process improvement projects, and in keeping with the project goals, the team identified specific training and professional development needs for the group, including business analysts. "An effective communication strategy and specific procedures for working with referrers that included checkpoints, exchanging client development information and otherwise ensuring that we continue to keep referrers "in the loop" with regard to clients entrusted to us were developed and implemented.

Additionally, standardized communications were established for consistency in messaging within the practice area and the firm. This includes simple but critical items such as file naming conventions across the practice area team and organizing data files in a highly specified file structure on a shared drive with standardized file names and email subjects. The new process also ensures that relevant information is stored on the firm's document management system and on a dedicated drive for practice group matters," says Nason.

The team also developed new practice group codes to better identify various components of practice area in order to measure profit, utilization, growth trends, and contractions. Another outcome of the project was established standard operating procedure of formalizing the relationship with the client on new matters, e.g. use of specific language (on documents such as engagement letters) to clarify details and logistics.

Following the project, the practice group took additional actions based on the team's recommendations. They engaged in strategic planning, where they developed core values and a mission statement to ensure that the team had a common purpose and was going in the same direction. Later, the practice group organized and conducted a two-day "boot camp" for all practice group members (attorneys, non-attorneys, administrator, and coordinator) to increase knowledge and train on the new processes.

The project also led them to establish a practice group administrator and coordinator. The administrator works directly with Nason as the practice group head on administrative matters, assigns analysts to prepare AAPs, monitors workflow and timeliness of AAP and audit preparation, interfaces with clients to respond to questions or triage them to attorneys, and serves as final quality control. The coordinator has assumed marketing and client service responsibilities that formerly were handled by the firm's client services group. This ensures that the practice group has a person with an intimate knowledge of their practice group services who is staffing exhibit booths and talking with clients (and potential clients) at conferences and seminars. The coordinator also sources various seminars for speaking opportunities

She is also responsible for quality control for AAP preparation. Both the practice group administrator and the coordinator are also timekeepers who bill hours. This project delivered important results: the practice group's fixed-fee AAPs are profitable; and they know which fixed fee arrangements are the most and least profitable. Also, OFCCP work is now delivered even more profitably and by an expanded team. Overall, they have increased the number of new matters over previous years, increased their billings and hours, and have robust and successful marketing.

Team member T. Scott Kelly, a shareholder who is also an active member of the American Bar Association's Section of Labor and Employment Law (where he currently is the employer co-chair of the Section's marketing committee), reflects on the OFCCP audit process improvement project his team delivered: "We initially sought to improve the manner in which we performed and delivered services to our clients. Our new process has increased our internal efficiencies, which we are able to pass along to our clients. These efficiencies are not confined to competitive pricing, which is a benefit, but also include precise and thoughtful client interactions."

Kelly goes on to point out, "Additionally, the Kaizen identified specific improvements to the interactions with lawyers in our firm that referred us work. Focusing on the manner, the content, and the amount of information we communicate with them has raised the referrers' level of satisfaction with our practice group. Another plus is the standardization of this process reduces the time involved in the process. So, we are keeping our clients and internal referrers happier, providing them more information, but with no loss to our own efficiencies."

Process improvement in litigation

Litigation is often an area in which it is initially more difficult to imagine how process improvement can be helpful. Two case studies that were published by Lisa Damon of Seyfarth Shaw in January 2014 are instructive in this regard.[1]

The first case study involved a retailer facing an increased number of personal injury lawsuits relating to store conditions "In each case, the plaintiff alleged unique facts that led to the injury. However, across the lawsuits, the facts about the stores were relatively consistent. Each lawsuit was covered by insurance if the costs to defend plus damages or settlement exceeded $250,000, but almost no cases were resolved above that threshold.

"At the inception of the process improvement program, the retailer faced more than 100 lawsuits, with an average cost per lawsuit of approximately $50,000. A combination of process improvement and project management, with the use of an AFA, helped the retailer manage its defense costs. In particular: Although the plaintiff's facts varied by lawsuit, the steps to defend were comparable. This allowed the legal team to consolidate tasks and develop a consistent approach. Through the AFA, the retailer achieved predictability for defense costs and incentivized outside counsel to increase efficiency in its practices. The integrated approach reduced the volume of lawsuits pending in the portfolio from approximately 100 at any given time to less than 10. The average cost per lawsuit also dropped from approximately $50,000 to less than $10,000. Overall, the retailer lowered its projected uninsured risk exposure from $5 million to $100,000."

The second case study included in Damon's article involved managing a litigation portfolio: "A large US defense contractor with multiple business units across the country needed a single law firm to handle its high volume of litigation and counseling needs. The client identified greater consistency in practices, quality of outcomes and efficiency as success targets for the legal team.

"Process improvement was key to meeting the client's objectives and delivering value. With input and support from the in-house lawyers, the selected law firm:

- Conducted extensive "voice of the client" interviews with corporate and division counsel to identify issues and potential root causes at the portfolio and matter levels.
- Developed a standard trial process map to assess each case for its potential to go to trial on the front end and throughout the case.
- Launched a new trial approach that triaged cases and staffing based on potential risk, with a flat fee AFA.

"The overall strategy led to improved outcomes and provided the client with greater predictability of its legal expenses. It created cost savings of 30% on an average per-matter basis for single-plaintiff employment litigation, based on a five-year track record of nearly 180 matters."

Increased efficiency and reduced errors at The Hunoval Firm

More recently, in March 2014, the American Bar Association Journal reported on The Hunoval Firm in North Carolina. This foreclosure firm believes in investing in deep skill development "by sending staff to training based on real projects being developed for the firm" and expects "a full 70% to be trained by the end of 2014". The ABA Journal article also mentions that the firm's "first project addressed the overly long process for a notice of hearing and achieved the impressive 88% timeline improvement."[2]

The firm says it has saved an estimated $4 million since 2012 through increased efficiencies, better timelines, and error reduction. It has, for instance, reduced the time it takes to file a North Carolina notice of hearing (NOH) from an average of 70 days to around eight.

"I knew that we would attain real operational benefits – increased efficiencies and reduction in errors – and it would help us run a better, more efficient law firm management," says Hunoval.[3] But, he adds, there were also a lot of unexpected benefits including workforce engagement and marketing.

Lean Six Sigma for mergers and acquisitions at Husch Blackwell

In his whitepaper "An Unconventional Alliance: Lessons from a Lean Six Sigma Pilot",[4] Lann Wasson of Husch Blackwell LLP reflects that "A complex mergers and acquisitions practice is an unlikely place to start a Lean Six Sigma pilot in a large law firm. Conventional wisdom would suggest that these methodologies from the manufacturing sector would more likely fit the operational side of the firm, as well as the more repetitive matters in commoditized practice areas. So in April 2010, when the chair of Husch Blackwell's mergers and acquisitions practice invited me to participate in a pilot to assist lawyers in using Lean Six Sigma on acquisitions, I knew that there would be many hours of work and challenges ahead for the whole team.

The genesis of the pilot started months earlier as lawyers in the firm began investigating different approaches to matter management, alternative fee pricing and a greater degree of leverage. While it was tempting to simply fine-tune existing approaches in an effort to control costs, these lawyers recognized that a new approach was needed to address the root causes of deal expense and client frustration. By identifying ways to achieve client goals more efficiently and effectively, the partners aimed to differentiate their services to ultimately give their clients a marketplace advantage and the firm greater market share.

Of the range of project management and process improvement methods available, the chair selected Lean Six Sigma as the pilot's frame of reference because these methodologies resonated with a cross section of the business community, including success in service sectors such as health care and banking. Furthermore, the tenets of Lean and Six Sigma, such as listening to clients, continuous improvement, process thinking and measurement, distinguished these approaches from others commonly used within the legal industry and promised to challenge status quo assumptions. Since the partners worked with different types of clients – from private equity investors to strategic buyers – the team needed an approach like Lean Six Sigma, which would allow them to develop their capability to collaborate with a client to design a framework that could improve its approach to deal management."

Capturing firm experience at Pillsbury

Opportunistically improving business processes can deliver excellent results as well. Kathleen T. Pearson is director of administration for Pillsbury's global operations center in Nashville, TN. The center houses the firm's global operations staff, including IT, human resources, document production, finance and accounting, as well as significant portions of the marketing department. Kathleen is responsible for managing all day-to-day functions of the 150+ person office and coordinating operational needs for attorneys throughout the firm's 14 other locations. A Six Sigma Green Belt, Legal Lean Sigma Yellow Belt, and graduate of George Washington University's Master's in Law Firm Management, Pearson is helping Pillsbury to achieve better efficiencies in firm operations.

While at Waller Lansden, Pearson delivered a process improvement project to capture firm experience that had a significant impact on operations and the firm's ability to understand and discuss its relevant experience with clients, prospects and referrers. The problem statement for the project was that the firm as not capturing its firm experience efficiently. Says Pearson, "Not having this information resulted in having to initiate a fire drill every time we needed specific experience for a proposal or client meeting; we ultimately were submitting incomplete information."

Her project included mapping the process in detail, which allowed her to identify specific issues and explore alternative "process designs" that eliminated waste and rework and educated employees. One improvement was that the firm created a useful tool in the form of a new data input screen. The result speaks for itself: the firm saw an improved capture of firm experience from 6 percent to 100 percent.

Combining opportunistic and systematic approaches

Since opportunistic approaches can dramatically differ, the examples can be found in many places along the continuum. For example, Gimbal Canada Inc. presented its 2013 work in a presentation to law students at the University of Ottawa in January 2014,[5] reporting that "Borden Ladner Gervais has mapped 30 processes (from litigation to M&A) and now uses its maps for training, KM and marketing." A different kind of success story included in the same presentation references a Virginia firm that "saved 30 hours and $21,000 by reducing set-up time in one afternoon, in the very first process they looked at".

Thompson Hine reports that it employs a combination of systematic and opportunistic approaches. The firm has invested heavily in resources, structure, and "air time", preaching the gospel of legal project management, process improvement, value billing, and staffing. The firm has dedicated resources, including its director of legal project management; its manager of pricing; working groups established to assist in successfully scoping, launching, managing and closing matters; and software, some of which was created by the firm, to model and optimize staffing, project milestones, budget, and actual spending, among other hard assets that have to be in place to truly succeed in integrating the rigors of matter management and efficiency in work. The firm is passionate about ingraining this approach firm-wide.

Acknowledging that vision doesn't come overnight, they couple the firm-wide effort with targeted opportunistic work. "Some matters present perfect circumstances for LPM, knowledge management tools, and alternative approaches to staffing. They are prime examples that can be held out for our lawyers to see the benefits of project management. Clients endorse these tools and love the results. The lawyers need to get on this bus," says Deborah Read, managing partner of Thompson Hine.

Thompson Hine notes five critical factors a firm needs to have in place to be successful as an opportunist:

1. Data – in the right form and accessible to the right people managing the matter;
2. An administrative team with the knowledge and bandwidth to create and support the legal team;
3. Basic tools to create the roadmap (client dialog, scope, work plan, reporting, ongoing dialog);
4. Impetus – whether internally derived or externally through the specifics of the engagement; and
5. A motivated partner who wants to lead with this approach.

Further, Thompson Hine outlines how those five critical success factors differ in order to be successful systematically across the firm:

1. Data – still an imperative, but the firm has to truly master the data;
2. Administrative team with the knowledge and bandwidth to create and support the legal team and an understanding of how tools and processes may need to be adapted to fit differing practices;
3. More sophisticated tools deployed firm-wide – technology underpinnings, collaboration tools, financial tools to model staffing and project management plans along with corresponding budget, ability to track spending, staffing deployment, matter project vs. budget, etc.;
4. Demonstrated reward for applying the approach – internal or external; and
5. Firm culture shift.

Everywhere in a law firm, there are processes that range from simple to complicated but all can be improved. Thomas L. Sager and Scott L. Winkelman, make the following recommendations:

- "Start with paper processes, which often lend themselves to standardized process improvements, and often yield quick victories;
- Map the process – mundane though it sounds, mapping often yields dramatic results by highlighting the process as it really exists;
- Target unconscious spending – staff often take action without even considering the costs;
- Apply information technology – IT fixes often bubble up early;
- Leverage the learning – multiply the benefits by leveraging project learning to similar processes and functions; and
- Be a forum for pent-up grievances – pent-up pet peeves are often the stuff of superb process improvement projects."[6]

The sequences and principles of Lean and Six Sigma are straightforward and clear. The logic of DMAIC, both in concept and application, begins to make more and more sense as law firms try to make their processes more efficient. There are many ways to select a first project but, if in doubt, your clients' feedback is an excellent place to get ideas about where to start.

References

1. Damon, L. "Applying Lean Six Sigma Methods to Litigation Practice" practice note, Practical Law, January 2014; see http://us.practicallaw.com/9-549-6388?q=&rqp-&rqo-&rqe-.
2. Carter, T., Foreclosure firm goes statistical to improve speed and quality, American Bar Association Journal online; www.abajournal. com/magazine/article/foreclosure_firm_ goes_statistical_to_improve_speed_and_ quality.
3. PEX, "CEO of Hunoval Law Firm: Lean Six Sigma was a 'lightbulb moment'"; see www.processexcellencenetwork.com/lean- six-sigma-business-transformation/articles/ six-sigma-in-law-interview-with-matt-hunoval.
4. Wasson, L. "An Unconventional Alliance: Lessons from a Lean Six Sigma Pilot", ILTA white paper, June 2011; see www.huschblackwell.com/~/media/Files/ BusinessInsights/BusinessInsights/2011/06/ ILTA%20White%20Paper%20An%20 Unconventional%20Alliance%20Less__/ Files/An%20Unconventional%20Alliance%20 Lessons%20from%20a%20Lean%20S__/FileAttachment/WassonILTA2011.pdf.
5. See http://gimbalcanada.com/professional- development.
6. Sager T.L., and Winkelman, S.L. "Six Sigma: Positioning for Competitive Advantage", ACCA Docket 19, No. 1, 2001.

Chapter 4:

Rethinking workflows: re-engineering case management processes

By Scott Rechtschaffen, chief knowledge officer, Littler Mendelson

Over two years ago, Littler Mendelson set out to re-engineer the way that they handle the defense of administrative agency charges for their clients. Starting with a challenge posed by a major client and a desire to re-engineer the way their legal services could be delivered, they successfully developed and deployed Littler CaseSmart.

CaseSmart is an innovative case management process that has garnered new business for the firm, earned awards and accolades, and produced several lessons about the right way to implement change within a large law firm. In the following case study, Scott Rechtschaffen shares how Littler radically changed its case management processes.

Challenge and opportunity

In early 2010, with the ongoing recession and legal departments across the country looking for ways to reduce their costs, the general counsel at one of our major clients asked all of its outside counsel to propose ways to reduce its annual legal spend. Fortunately for Littler and, equally important, for the client, the shareholder responsible for managing the firm's work for the client saw this as an opportunity, not an obstacle.

At the time, Littler was handling about 25 percent of that client's administrative agency charges (i.e. charges filed with the federal Equal Employment Opportunity Commission or state agencies alleging, among other things, discrimination, harassment, or retaliation).

Recognizing that, for large employers, administrative agency charges have become commodity work – while some charges may have merit, many are the employment law equivalent of slip-and-fall nuisance filings – the shareholder wondered whether he could propose handling all of the client's administrative charges nationwide (over 1,000 charges annually) for a flat per-charge fee that would reduce the client's per-charge legal spend and its overall legal spend using multiple law firms, as it had been doing.

Reviewing the economics of the hundreds of charges our firm had handled for that client over the years and relying on the "law of large numbers", he calculated that a flat per-charge fee would enable the firm to balance those work-intensive cases (i.e. where the firm would lose money) against the charges that could be handled more expediently. However, handling this volume of charges profitably would require a much more efficient process than the firm had at the time.

The shareholder did not want to simply outsource portions of the work or to push the work down to the lowest-level associates; the firm's longstanding relationship with the client depended on ensuring the highest quality work product and results – even on commodity work.

The proposal would have to demonstrate that we had a plan to ensure the work product and results – as well as the client's relationship with the federal and state agencies – would not suffer.

The proposal would also have to demonstrate that this was not just a loss leader, an effort to get the client's higher value work; the shareholder knew that this client would see through and reject such an approach as not sustainable over the long run.

Creating a new approach

We quickly brought together a small team to assess the technology and alternative staffing solutions that would be needed to make the proposal viable. This initial working group consisted of attorneys intimately familiar with the client and several of the firm's C-level executives. We also brought in some outside technology consultants that were already working with the firm on other projects.

The CaseSmart approach developed by our team consisted of four main components:

1. A comprehensive process-flow analysis of administrative agency charge work;
2. A proprietary case management technology platform;
3. An alternative staffing model; and
4. Transparent access to all cases for the client.

1. Process-flow analysis

Our CaseSmart team brought together a number of the firm's subject matter experts experienced in handling administrative agency charges in a series of meetings.

Working with technologists and business analysts, we developed a step-by-step work-process map of how most attorneys manage the defense of administrative agency charges, from the moment the charge is received by the client to the point at which the matter is finally closed – whether by a settlement or a decision by the agency that is either favorable or adverse to the employer.

2. Proprietary platform

Based on the work-process analysis, and working with both in-house applications developers and outside consultants, we developed and deployed an advanced, proprietary case management platform designed to streamline and automate many of the steps required to process and manage charges.

A charge-intake process was developed to enable highly skilled administrators to enter into the system pertinent information that the attorneys handling the charges would need ready access to, such as:

1. Biographical data concerning the charge;
2. The alleged actors and the witnesses;
3. The pertinent facts and legal theories set forth in the charge; and
4. Personnel information pulled from the client's HR systems.

We then deployed document automation software to automate the production of standard, repetitive documents and also workflow tools to enable better case management and tracking of work product and deadlines.

We also developed a comprehensive Microsoft SharePoint TeamSite that would enable working attorneys to readily access client information, legal research, and template documents, and to communicate efficiently using social networking tools.

The overall platform was designed to enable attorneys to work more efficiently and to ensure overall quality and performance standards were maintained.

3. Alternative staffing model

Our team had analyzed the work processes, identifying inefficiencies. We had looked for:

- Tasks being performed by shareholders that could be performed by associates;

- Tasks being performed by associates that administrative staff could perform; and
- Tasks administrative staff were performing that technology should be handling.

Based on this analysis, we recognized that the traditional shareholder-associate-secretary model of handling a matter would not enable the type of efficient task-based process we envisioned; we knew that CaseSmart would require an alternative staffing model.

The first step was to develop the highly skilled administrative staff that could perform the intake and initial discovery processes effectively and also oversee case management.

The next step was to recruit a cadre of flex-time attorneys (FTA) with substantial experience in handling administrative charges and who desired an alternative career path that included flexibility and greater control over their schedules and caseloads. We decided early on that these FTAs would be staff attorneys, not outsourced or contract attorneys.

One of our reasons for using FTAs, as opposed to traditional associates, was that FTAs could be deployed in a task-based, team structure; they would only work on CaseSmart charges and they would be dedicated to specific clients.

In this way, they would become extremely proficient at performing a specific set of tasks – investigating and defending administrative agency charges – and they would get to know their assigned client's culture, operational issues, and personnel extremely well, thus greatly increasing their efficiency.

A team of responsible supervising attorneys (RSA) – shareholders experienced in working with specific clients – would supervise the FTAs, assisting them in performing a risk analysis. This is a critical step in determining early on whether the charge should be settled or defended, based on parameters defined by the client in advance.

The RSAs would also be responsible for reviewing the FTAs' work product, particularly statements of position submitted to the agency in defense of the employer's position.

Finally, each client would be assigned an overall project director to oversee the work of the administrative team, the FTAs, and the RSAs, and to be the client's primary point of contact for overall case management issues.

4. Matter transparency

One of the keys to the CaseSmart system is that it is an outsourced model: the client effectively turns over management of individual charge matters to our firm, enabling the client to focus, instead, on how we are handling its overall caseload. This eliminates the inefficiencies that arise from back-and-forth decision-making on individual charges, enabling the client to deploy its internal legal team to handle higher-value matters.

But, to make this model work, the client has to have the management tools necessary to monitor how effectively the overall caseload is being handled. The client needs to feel confident that individual cases are not languishing, that the firm is not settling too many cases or spending too much on settlements, and that the quality of the work product meets the standards the client expects.

To enable the client to monitor these critical issues, the system was designed to provide transparent access through an online dashboard that enables the client to see the status of any given matter – the charge data, agency documents, and the attorney's work product – as well as to see the status of all of its matters at a macro level.

It enables clients to see real-time key performance indicators showing, amongst other things, the number of charges being settled versus the number of charges being defended, the average settlement amount, and the length of time it takes to resolve charges.

More importantly, the dashboard provides clients with actionable intelligence about what is going on within their own organizations. Clients can see the types of claims being filed and the location of these claims (such as regions or facilities that are encountering larger numbers of charges), enabling them to make informed operational decisions (such as which regions or facilities require additional management training or which internal policies might require review and revision).

Lessons learned

Our approach has proven successful on many levels. Over the past two years, we have managed more than 3,400 administrative agency charges through the system, exceeding expectations in terms of quality of work product and results, efficiency, cost savings to the clients, and realization for the firm.

Our firm has brought new clients onto the system and has garnered industry accolades and industry honors, including the International Legal Technology Association's 2011 project of the year award and the 2012 InnovAction award from the College of Law Practice Management.

While the accolades and the new business are, of course, tremendously rewarding, the success of the project has provided an opportunity to re-evaluate what really works in terms of legal process re-engineering and how law firms can adjust to the "new normal" for delivering legal services.

What follows are just a few of the lessons we learned from the CaseSmart project.

1. It really does take a village to implement meaningful change

While our initial team consisted of a small core group, the real operational team would eventually involve over 60 individuals across virtually every corporate department in the firm and five outside technology providers.

For example, initial operational plans were adjusted once our chief information security officer and his team got involved and focused on the need to ensure client data was effectively protected, particularly with FTAs working remotely. Specific security precautions were implemented to ensure data security at every step in the process.

Our chief product officer and his team helped to develop the processes followed by the administrative team to ensure the efficient processing of client information.

The professional development staff were instrumental in designing a program to ensure the FTAs were integrated into the firm's training and development programs.

Our finance and accounting department was critical in developing protocols to ensure there is meaningful case management reporting for both the firm's and the client's benefit.

2. Support from firm leadership is critical

From the very beginning, our management committee and senior leadership recognized the possibilities of the project and the potential future impact the project could have on the way we deliver legal services.

Indeed, our chief operating officer was a member of the CaseSmart leadership team from the outset and was involved in most of the major decision-making throughout the development phase.

3. Think big, start small

Any effort to entirely re-engineer the way a large well-established firm does business will encounter insurmountable obstacles. A better approach is to focus on a small area of the firm's practice, demonstrate success, and offer to replicate that success in other areas.

We were able to take one process (the management of administrative agency charges), improve it significantly, and show it as a successful model for other areas of practice. Other practice groups have since requested help with re-engineering the way that they deliver legal services.

We are now looking at applying our CaseSmart approach to single plaintiff litigation, wage-hour class actions, and other aspects of the labor and employment practice group.

4. The "new normal" poses challenges, but also opportunities

Many attorneys have confronted the dramatic changes in the legal industry by hoping that the good old days of ever-rising rates and limited client pushback will return.

The firms that will have the greatest success in the new paradigm, however, will realize that the good old days are not coming back and they must try equally dramatic approaches to re-thinking their business strategies. By doing so, they can find new ways of generating increased revenue, realization, and profitability, as well as delivering greater value to their clients.

Key takeaway points:

1. It really does take a village to implement meaningful change, so plan to include all relevant people early on;
2. Support from the firm's management committee and senior leadership is critical;
3. Think big, start small – Focus on a small area of a firm's practice, demonstrate success, and offer to replicate that success in other areas; and
4. The "new normal" poses challenges but also opportunities – Consider dramatic approaches when rethinking your business strategies.

A version of this chapter first appeared in Managing Partner magazine in January 2013.

About the author

As chief knowledge officer of Littler Mendelson P.C., Scott D. Rechtschaffen leads the firm's effort to provide innovative client services by integrating new technologies and work processes, and enabling attorneys and clients to access the collective knowledge and experience of the firm's more than 1,000 attorneys. He combines over 25 years of experience representing companies in every area of labor and employment law with a broad understanding of technology to help the firm's attorneys and their clients in tailoring unique solutions that enhance the firm's ability to deliver legal information and legal services to its clients.

Scott heads the firm's knowledge management (KM) department comprising dedicated, full-time knowledge management attorneys – who are all experienced employment and labor law attorneys, technologists, research specialists, and administrative support. The KM team supports the firm's attorneys, practice groups, and major firm initiatives. He has been a key member of the multi-disciplinary team that developed the award-winning Littler CaseSmart® approach to legal case management. He oversees KM's work on the firm's electronic and print publications – The National Employer, blogs and newsletter alerts, Smart Search – the firm's internal search engine, LittlerNet – the firm's intranet portal, Littler's Extranets, and online subscription services – Littler GPS® and Littler Monitor.

In addition, Scott is responsible for the firm's Executive Employer® Conference, an annual gathering of in-house counsel and human resources professionals representing some of the country's leading organizations. He was the co-creator of Winning Through Prevention: The Littler Employment Law Challenge, an innovative teaching tool designed to enhance the training of managers and supervisors. Scott has written extensively and has published articles in national publications on human resources management, knowledge management, and legal technology. He regularly speaks at knowledge management seminars and legal technology conferences organized by the American Bar Association's Law Practice Management Section, Association of Corporate Counsel, American Lawyer Media, Legal Marketing Association, International Legal Technology Association, ARK Group, and other professional organizations.

Chapter 5: Data-driven knowledge management – matter lifecycle management

By Chad Ergun, director, global practice services and business intelligence at Gibson, Dunn & Crutcher LLP

We are living in an era of big data, promoted by low-cost storage and cloud computing, with the promise of advanced algorithms and increased adoption of internet of things (IoT). When combined with artificial intelligence, machine learning, and data visualization tools, these new solutions create the perfect breeding conditions for big data. Gartner defines "big data" as high-volume, high-velocity, and high-variety information assets that demand cost-effective, innovative forms of information processing for enhanced insight and decision making. Big data has yet another layer for advanced decision processing or decision support systems (DSS) called big data analytics. Big data analytics is the process of examining big data to uncover hidden patterns, unknown correlations, and other useful information that can be used to make better decisions. With big data analytics, data scientists and other specialists can analyze high volumes of data that conventional analytics or traditional business intelligence platforms cannot handle.

Big data is defined by the four dimensions of volume, velocity, variety, and value. These four Vs may be elaborated upon further as follows:

- **Volume:** Machine-generated data that is produced in much larger quantities than non-traditional data;
- **Velocity:** This refers to the speed of data processing, or the low latency rate at which analytics must be applied to the data, and looped back to the original sources of data to action;
- **Variety:** This refers to the large variety of input data (customer insights, competitive intelligence, trends, benchmarking data, standards, materials, etc.), which in turn generates a large variety of data as output; and

- **Value:** The economic value of different data varies significantly depending upon both the source and its end use. Firms must be clear at the outset about the business value big data initiatives will bring.

The rapid use of electronics and IT in products during the last two decades has resulted in many organizations sitting on an enormous amount of data – direct and indirect and/or past and present. Most IT systems used for product design, analysis, engineering, testing, and validation processes generate a large volume and variety of data. The increasing proliferation of computers and embedded electronics in the manufacturing industry, particularly in the automotive segment, has further resulted in the generation of a huge amount of structured and unstructured data. For example, use of computers and sensors in modern vehicles generates enormous data while a vehicle is in use.

The emerging challenge for organizations is to derive meaningful insights from available data and re-apply it intelligently. Knowledge management plays a crucial role in efficiently managing this data and delivering it to the end users to aid in the product development process. This involves collection of data from direct and indirect sources, analyzing and synthesizing it along with relevant enterprise data to derive meaningful information and intelligence, converting it into a useful knowledge base, storing it, and finally delivering it to end users.

To derive the maximum benefit from big data, organizations must modify their IT infrastructure to handle the rapid rate of delivery and extraction of huge volumes of data, with varying data types. These can then be integrated with the organization's enterprise data and analyzed. In fact, organizations, especially those with legacy systems, need to have a clear understanding of their past data and how the same can be merged into their current IT systems.

According to Yuan, Yoon, and Helendar, knowledge areas are classified into four types, collectively referred to as M-H-T-P: market knowledge, human knowledge, technology knowledge, and procedural knowledge. Based on these four knowledge areas, Table 1 depicts the mapping with elements of big data in the product development process.

Knowledge type	Volume	Velocity	Variety	Value
Market knowledge	• Customer data • Competitor data	• Direct interactions • Social media • Surveys	• Market analysis • Demographic data • Benchmarking data • Trends	• High value • Customer data • Competitor data
Human knowledge	• Experience based • Collaborative	• Real-time decision making	• Skill based • Experience based • Tacit knowledge	• Heuristic
Technology knowledge	• Standards • Usage • Materials • Field data	• Safety • Real-time data acquisition	• Cost • Reliability • Packaging • Ergonomics, etc.	• Patents
Procedural knowledge	• Design knowledge • Analysis • Materials std. • Verification, testing, and validation of knowledge	• Design knowledge • Std. materials library	• Design • CAD/CAM/CAE • Analysis • Manufacturing	• CAD/CAM/CAE data • Best practices • Test and validation • Service data • Manufacturing process data

Table 1: M-H-T-P

Knowledge management and big data

Big data has become so ubiquitous and integrated into our daily lives that it is expected to have significant effect on knowledge harvesting and sharing within an organization. The promised benefits of big data analytics combined with low cost, on-premises storage and cloud computing (lack of information governance notwithstanding), has created a data tsunami for many organizations. The first wave has hit e-discovery and resulted in significantly increased litigation and investigation costs. In response, e-discovery vendors have pushed back with advanced case analytics and case assessment tools in order to offer more predictability. The second wave is now about to revolutionize not only litigation or transactional practitioners, but overall matter lifecycle management (MLM), ranging from business intake to information governance and knowledge management.

Some of the early law firm adopters of big data analytics are adding chief data scientists (CDSs) to their KM teams and building data science teams to control the second wave of the data tsunami by using technology. Under the heavy pressure of technology advancements in data collection and processing, the conventional way of thinking about knowledge management for professional services is rapidly evolving.

Not long ago, the human element was a vital ingredient of big data analytics due to limitations within data science. We are now seeing impressive research results from MIT and technology vendors in replacing human intuition in pattern recognition by predicting and revealing those patterns. The same model applies to knowledge harvesting, collection, and distribution.

Some of the significant, but time consuming and costly, tasks of KM can be handled by big data analytics, pattern recognition algorithms, and machine learning systems. Instead of the push from professional support lawyers (PSLs) and resource attorneys, the new method could pull valuable data from different repositories using the technologies mentioned above to provide proactive solutions to fee earners and their clients. A well-designed strategy to support such a solution requires the ability to sense, acquire, transmit, process, store, and analyze the data to generate knowledge and distribute through different channels.

Law firm adoption

Law firms can utilize big data and KM in several areas: legal research, e-discovery, business intelligence, practice development, client sentiment analysis, budgeting, and financial planning.

1. **Learning from past practices:** A good place for firms to start is to make use of the historic data they already possess. Unfortunately, those are often in non-digitized form. Scanning old case documents, notes, and records can open a world of potential data that can be analyzed to give added depth to the firm's understanding of typical cases and practice matters.
2. **Client satisfaction rankings:** If a firm is trying to better understand clients' levels of satisfaction with the firm's services, email data is probably a good starting point. At the moment, email is the largest form of most unstructured firm data. Big data analytics can be used to survey things like client reactions, matter closing checklists, and billing-related issues. They can identify emotional responses to client communications, identifying words or phrases that negatively impact clients' acceptance of bills, or measure overall tone of the written communications.
3. **Speeding-up e-discovery:** Many e-discovery vendors tout the use of big data for improving overall experience and cost reduction.

Computer-assisted discovery is already the norm accepted by federal and state agencies. The addition of big data tools has the potential to make the process even more efficient. For example, it can increase the accuracy of predicting responsive documents and addressing investigation requests from government agencies. Some of these new tools can even be used for facial expression analysis that can then be utilized during mock trials to train litigators for the jury selection process. The same type of software has been used in the past with an audience watching the presidential debate to determine the "winner". McDonald's has also used it to determine how employees' moods affected the moods of its customers.

4. **Legal research:** The legal research and knowledge management tasks are excellent candidates for big data analytics. The true value of these analytics tools can be measured by introducing metrics to capture reactive and proactive legal research. Legal research fed by big data, internal KM repositories, and third-party content providers can easily provide a proactive platform to address fee-earners' needs before they ask for such information. A good example is a product called Ross, the world's first "digital attorney" powered by IBM Watson, which was developed by a group of students at the University of Toronto. Lawyers using Ross ask a legal question, and the program sifts through thousands of legal documents, statutes, and cases to provide an answer. Ross's responses include legal citations, suggest articles for further reading, and even calculate a confidence rating to help lawyers prepare for cases. Because Ross is a cognitive computing platform, it learns from past interactions, meaning that Ross's responses will grow to be more accurate as lawyers continue to use its system.

Matter lifecycle management

About six years ago, as a consultant, I was invited to attend a special committee meeting headed by a managing partner of a law firm to discuss practice technologies and major challenges facing fee earners. Surrounded by brilliant legal minds heading different practice areas, I asked if they could estimate average costs for different types of deals and engagements in various jurisdictions. I collected and shared their responses on-screen, showing three charts comparing the answers from practice heads, financial systems, and numbers based on my assessment. Needless to say, they were all different numbers. When I pitched the idea of technology-assisted matter budgeting, I was told by a transactional practice head that the process is hunch-based and does not require technology due to the complexity involved in calculating not only the direct cost but also in estimating potential risks and challenges.

Fast forward to 2015, and we are now dealing with a vast collection of data, armed with advanced technology, and working with millennials as fee earners. Due to the low cost of storage and need for data-driven decision systems, we are also hoarding data and storing transactional information. This new approach is making its way into our daily lives and is mostly observed as new technology in the consumer market. Major corporations, on the other hand, utilize the big data/advanced algorithms/artificial intelligence trio to cut costs, better understand human behavior, and make data-driven decisions. Examples range from parcel delivery companies tracking driver brake positions with GPS coordinates for better route management, to utilizing a large number of medical images for detecting diseases.

There are now specific applications riding this new wave of technology at law firms too. Some of them focus on e-discovery and litigation case management, and others target transactional practices. Using advanced case analytics and case assessment tools are becoming popular approaches for internal investigations and other e-discovery-related projects. Due to the highly complex nature of the legal process involved in litigation cases, cost predictability has become a major game changer. Unfortunately, costs for document review and e-discovery processes are adversely impacted by large volumes of content (another side-effect of data hoarding and cheap storage).

E-discovery technologies such as analytics for culling, early case assessment, and relevancy review are introducing major cost savings. Some companies are taking proactive measures and apply information governance (IG) to reduce data clutter, activate retention policies, and streamline content flow within their organizations. A well-established IG workflow significantly reduces the volume of documents and emails subject to discovery and review, providing substantial savings in both e-discovery costs and effort.

Similar technology and process re-engineering opportunities exist on the transactional side and are becoming more noteworthy. Fee earners working on corporate deals expect more predictive technology involvement in tracking their deals. They want automated notifications and better control over matter workflow. Other functions that can better utilize technology are deal budgeting, billing, and legal research.

Unlike the cost savings opportunities motivating litigators and clients for e-discovery, the initiatives focusing on transactional deals are more complicated to justify and show clear ROIs. When combined with lack of mainstream commercial products or supporting content, most of these initiatives cannot reach the production cycle for adoption by practicing attorneys.

So, how can we take advantage of big data, advanced technology, and information governance to address the needs of both transactional and litigation attorneys? The answer is a data-driven MLM platform with advanced algorithms and rich content harvested from big data initiatives. The concept behind MLM is very simple: track your deals and cases using advanced predictive technology and combine it with transactional data that used to be discarded. The concept of tracking matters from inception to closing is not new, and it does not require advanced technology, expensive tools, or major investment.

Pitch phase

MLM starts with the pitch phase as a pre-intake activity. During this stage, pitches and proposals are put together based on past experience and similar deals, and are tailored to address clients' specific needs. Matter budgeting and staffing are other elements to consider at this point as well. In a fully populated MLM platform, the past experience, budget/cost analysis, profitability margins, fee-earner utilizations, and staffing analysis should be available to marketing staff and partners.

In addition to gathering data for a pitch or proposal, tracking the outcome of this phase is crucial and needs to be saved in the MLM platform. Authorized parties can search the collection and locate historical data about successful – or unsuccessful – proposals, better understand the clients' decision-making criteria, and build a trend analysis comparing the target to others in the same market and/or jurisdiction.

Relying on your CRM system and a collection of past pitches or proposals is no longer an industry best practice and does not provide competitive advantage over your competitors in the marketplace. Unfortunately, highly dynamic pricing models combined with shifting priorities and complex legal issues require an intelligent platform that updates itself based on each experience, activity, and response. Such an approach will help big law firms to introduce algorithmic marketing and provide more powerful solutions to partners, business development, and marketing staff.

Opening phase

After the completion of a successful pitch phase, a new matter and/or client intake phase starts based on the data gathered from the initial set of activities. The suggested best practice is to have a fully automated new business intake (NBI) workflow in place for this MLM phase.

The details captured can be included in the NBI to start the process, and are updated when the intake phase is complete. Relevant information can then be published on an internal intranet site for each client and matter. The opening phase integrates with other platforms such as finance, human resources, professional development, marketing, and training. Each end point for the NBI workflow can be monitored with automated notifications to ensure proper handling of new clients and matters. In addition to the audit trail created for compliance purposes, the same workflow can also provide KPIs to measure the time to open a new client/matter and detect any unusual delays in the process. These advanced processes built into the NBI workflow will reduce delays, and increase efficiency and utilization. The matters that are subject to confidentiality can be tagged at this phase and only made visible to the timekeepers of the matter team.

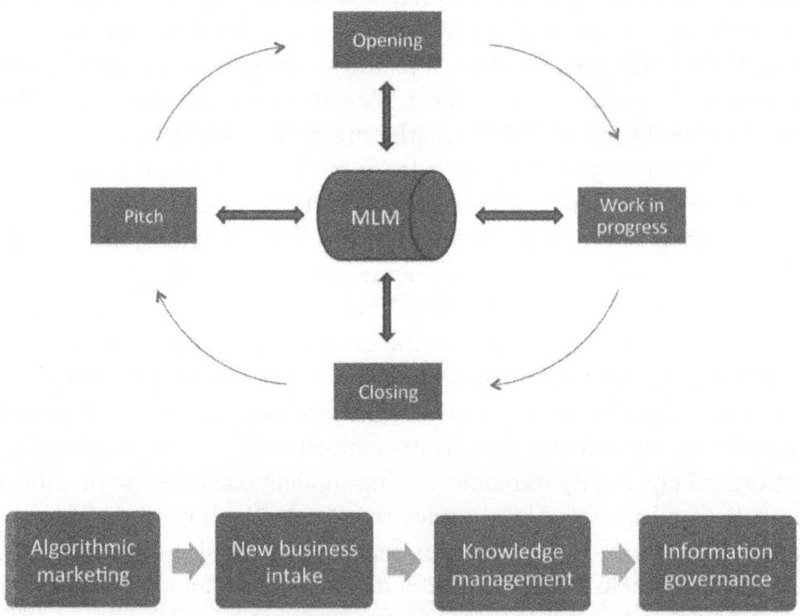

Figure 1: MLM workflow

Work in progress

The third step of MLM is the work in progress (WIP) phase. At this stage, proper client/matter numbers are already assigned, all conflict checks are completed, and related documentation such as engagement letters and billing guidelines are uploaded into the system. All activities in this phase can be pushed to the MLM platform for each matter and published on their intranet sites with appropriate security. It is here where KM plays a major role in helping attorneys locate actionable content, model documents, and precedents. Some of the most visible practice technologies such as knowledge libraries, enterprise search, predictive coding, legal project management, research, and other KM solutions are used by fee earners.

An algorithm-based proactive decision workflow can be used to direct attorneys and their support staff to a correct set of resources and improve legal research activities. Some of the other approaches include sharing matter updates and relevant documents with clients by utilizing automated notifications. You can also take advantage of big data, news feeds, and social media updates to trigger alerts to notify all parties involved in specific deals. Any unusual activity can be monitored to prevent unauthorized content modification, access, and other audit elements.

Closing

The last phase of MLM is the matter closing. This stage can be triggered by pre-set threshold variables such as number of hours billed, uploading deal closing sets, or direct updates from the partner in charge of the matter. The system can initiate automated matter closing notifications to alert authorized parties and obtain final approval to star the matter closing tasks. Once the closing is finalized, the retention cycle based on IG rules is initiated. Depending on variables included in the deal profiles, certain matters can be released to internal resources. The closing phase also involves the records department as the last stop for executed documents for recordkeeping purposes.

After a successful implementation of MLM with advanced analytics, you should be able to:

- Search deals based on location, industry, or closing value and combine that with attorney expertise and availability to build matter teams;

- Create matter budgets within 5–10 percent accuracy range;
- Locate valuable KM content such as precedents based on deal profile search;
- Receive alerts when an unusual activity is detected within the MLM workflow;
- Get daily summary updates about active matters and content shared with clients and other third parties; and
- Set up custom alerts to monitor major milestones.

The value of MLM

MLM processes can enable law firms to fully integrate predictive technologies that streamline client-matter workflow, resource management, budgeting, and legal project management. But a mature MLM will require well-designed new business intake (NBI), information governance (IG), and actionable content. Without these pillars to support the process, MLM will fail in the long term.

On the technology side, MLM needs to offer a proactive approach with advanced features and intelligent workflow to get fee earners engaged. For example, receiving alerts while drafting a credit agreement that precedents or similar content already exists in your KM library. Actionable intelligence combined with behavioral analytics will bring significant value to MLM and will improve the overall user experience.

Historically, law firms are not early adopters of advanced technology due to a potentially high risk-to-benefit ratio and lack of R&D resources, but we are now facing unprecedented force and velocity of disruptive technologies. These new solutions (such as Watson-like artificial intelligence tools, predictive coding, decision-making algorithms, big data with visualization, and cloud-based SaaS), combined with cost-cutting efforts resulting from the financial crisis, are early indications of a new era. Believe it or not, the legal industry is in the midst of an analytics revolution. Some of the early adopters are building data science teams and are hiring chief data scientists (CDS) to control the explosion of big data by using technology. Others are already using these technologies on a daily basis during case review and early case assessment, or for document review with predictive coding.

Currently, hunch and gut-feelings are the dominant decision-making methods in the corporate world. If you are in a volatile market facing rapidly changing variables, relying on judgment calls based on past experience is becoming increasingly unreliable. However, exclusively depending on big data analytics and science will block your long-term vision and force you to make reactive and short-term decisions. Therefore, you need a decision-making approach that combines the key elements of data analytics with past management experience. This is where MLM plays a major role, offering lawyers, business development, and marketing staff a new way to profile, track, and search deals. Most importantly, it offers them a new way to make data-driven decisions.

Chapter 6:
Taking knowledge management to a strategic level

By Keith Lipman, progenitor of Matter Centricity and co-founder of Prosperoware, and Toby Brown, chief practice officer at Akin Gump

Single-digit growth since 2008 – with no real uptick in sight – is driving large law firms to develop parallel strategies: one focused on finding new ways to grow; and one focused on operational efficiency. This state of the industry represents an opportunity for knowledge management professionals to play a strategic role in the law firm. Once the easy steps for operational efficiency are taken, typically "right-sized" staffing models and better use of office space, firms will take a hard look at their real pain points: fee predictability and a true understanding of matter economics. For that they will need *you* (although they may not know it yet). You and your ability to leverage existing work product and share collective know how. You and your ability to connect your knowledge management strategy to your firm's core business strategies and bottom line.

It won't be easy. We're an old industry and change occurs slowly. But you *can* affect change. You *can* play a meaningful role in the firm's transition to the new reality we all do business in. And you *will* be recognized for it. Let's take a look at what you need to know to make that happen.

What you need to know about the state of the industry

How did we get here? The impact of the 2008 recession took everyone by surprise and upended the legal profession as we knew it. Law-firm clients have become increasingly "cost conscious". They're looking more closely at service specifics: Are we really spending $60,000 in legal services for a $60,000 contract? They're often turning to alternative providers in pursuit of cost efficiencies: legal process outsourcers for due diligence and third-party e-discovery companies for document review. Some clients are choosing to hire more legal staff and manage their legal work themselves, essentially using a law firm as a subcontractor instead of a prime. Demands for discounts, alternative fees, and tightly managed hourly rates are a common occurrence: anything clients deem a way to get better value is fair game.

For many law firms, these trends have created a meaningful drop in demand with everyone fighting for a share of the market. This, in turn, has made the legal services industry hypercompetitive, intensifying the imperative for fundamental change in the service models law firms employ today. Alternative fee arrangements, in particular, are under the spotlight.

News flash! Alternative fee arrangements come in many disguises

While almost all law firms have taken steps to get leaner with fewer support staff and tighter margins, many people feel their firm is not under pressure because their number of alternative fee arrangements is low. Many fail to realize that clients who are tightly managing hourly rates and the billing process are creating the equivalent of alternative fee arrangements.

Let's take a simple example of what savvy clients are doing to ensure greater bang for their buck. In a typical scenario, the client first negotiates a discount on the rates and asks the partner for a budget. Then, they tightly monitor each invoice: is there any work on here that didn't add value? Is any of this work due to inefficiencies? Is every charge within the scope of what we asked for? Are they staying within budget? The result: the matter effectively becomes an alternative fee arrangement. Based on this fact, many prefer to call alternative fee arrangements and highly discounted hourly matters "non-standard fee arrangements".

What you need to know about basic firm economics

Both standard and non-standard arrangements demand price control and a basic knowledge of firm economics. Let's look at what you need to know about profit models and profit drivers to play a more strategic role in your firm.

Like everything in our industry, how we measure profits has significantly changed. Until recently, law firm profits were built into their pricing model. The billable hour was enough to cover costs and a rising profit margin. It was easy to measure profit though a simple understanding of discount from the standard or headline rate. So long as the discount was not too much, the firm made money.

This approach worked well, and firms built a compensation system that reflected that every dollar coming in the door was a good one. No longer. A new model is emerging where profits need to be truly measured at a matter level. Two partners – each having a $5 million book of business – could have radically different levels of profitability. Today, the factors that drive margins are front and center in law firms. The most important profit drivers are rates, collected realization, productivity, and leverage.

Rates are a profit driver

Although this may be obvious, the point still needs to be made: billing rates are the core pricing structure used in the legal industry, and the level of a firm's rates is key in determining its level of profitability. As a rule of thumb, a one-point increase in rates leads to a two-point increase in profit. The reverse applies as well. In our experience, firms typically have a range of 1–3 percent increase in profit for each point of rate change. The range exists because it depends on the specific timekeepers involved and the relationship between the billing rates and the timekeepers' cost rates.

Collected realization is a profit driver

Realization is the percentage of money collected versus the standard rate. Once you have a standard rate, there are three basic factors that drive down the actual dollars collected against that rate: discounts, write-downs, and write-offs. Adding these three components together gives you total realization. The final number is important, but the three components are instructive for helping you understand what's driving a level of realization.

The impact of realization is much the same as that of rates. A 1 percent drop in realization will, on average, result in a 2 percent drop in profitability (at least it does when you are relatively close to 100 percent realization). As that realization number drops, the impact magnifies. When you approach 60–70 percent realization, it becomes infinite because you are approaching the cost-rate levels of most timekeepers. In other words, you are reaching the point where your margin goes to zero. When you pass that point, it goes to negative. At a general level, the point-of-no-return is about 67 percent. However, it can vary based on the mix of timekeepers involved in a given piece of work. Some timekeeper's cost rates can be 50 percent of billing rates; others may be closer to 80 percent.

Let's look at the components of collected realization a little more deeply:

- **Discounts.** Discounts happen when the market (in the form of our clients) tells us our prices are too high for particular pieces of work.

You might think firms should lower their prices in response to this information, but that could be a mistake. Sometimes clients shop price by the level of discounts they can get. In other words, they are not concerned with the actual price as much as they are focused on the dollar amount of the discount they can extract. Whether this is rational behavior in an economic sense is not relevant. Firms need to adjust their pricing and pricing strategies in response to the market. To counter this behavior, many firms raise their headline rate so they can provide the discount without effect.

- **Write-downs.** Write-downs are reductions from a bill before it goes to the client. This reduction signals that the firm or a partner has decided that a particular effort had no value. Examples of this include: the work is out-of-scope and the partner knows the client will not pay for it; the associate was inefficient in their work; or the associate did not understand the assignment and did the wrong thing. This becomes important as firms look for ways to lower the cost of delivering a service. By identifying recurring types of write-downs and eliminating the effort before the work is performed, a firm can lower the cost of the service.
- **Write-offs.** Write-offs are reductions requested by the client after they have seen the bill. Write-offs signal that the client did not see value in a particular effort. This may occur because the firm did not communicate the value of the effort properly, or it may just be that the work should not have been done. Note that, in some cases, write-offs are just good old-fashioned flaky clients who don't pay their bills – a cost of doing business.

Productivity is a profit driver

Productivity (aka utilization) is the number of billed hours per timekeeper. Most firms will have a benchmark productivity of 1,800 to 2,000 billable hours per year, driving an expectation of a certain baseline level of productivity. For profitability, this comes into play in cost rates.

Each timekeeper has a cost per year. There are two components of cost: compensation and overhead, commonly referred to as direct (compensation) and indirect (overhead) costs. The indirect costs are usually a hot-button issue for firms, often resulting in intense debates about where various administrative costs should be applied. Side-stepping that issue in our discussion, firms decide on reasonable numbers based on the level of the timekeepers. Partners, for instance, may have higher overhead cost allocations because they use more resources. Once a firm agrees on these costs, you divide the overall cost number by the benchmark number of hours to get a cost rate per hour.

The punch line on productivity: When productivity goes down, cost rates go up. If you have a lawyer who costs $500,000 per year working 1,900 hours, her cost is $263 per hour. If her productivity drops to 1,700 hours, her cost rate increases to $294 per hour.

The impact of cost rate changes on profit is typically half that of realization. Of course, that depends on the differential between the cost rate and the realized rate. The closer they are, the bigger the impact, and it becomes just like the point-of-no-return seen in realization.

Leverage is a profit driver

The authors often think of leverage as the "great equalizer". Leverage is the amount of non-partner work versus partner work performed or, from another angle, the percentage of partner time worked per matter or per client. We take this tangent for an important reason. Leverage is the highest-impact profit driver. When firms want to enhance their profitability, they will encourage the best use of leverage and not let low productivity promote counter-productive behavior.

The basic economic concept of leverage is that the more workers work, the more owners (partners) benefit. Workers generate the profits that pay partners. Therefore, the more work pushed down to them, the better leverage the firm has, and the more profit is generated.

Of course, caveats apply. Partner-level work should be done by a partner. The mantra here is: push work down to its lowest cost while using the appropriate labor source. This sounds obvious and reasonable. However, until recently, firms have profited from pushing work up to the highest-rate source, which was a great idea when competition was low.

Taken to a logical extreme, you could make the argument that partners should do no work to maximize profits. Technically, you would be correct. If partners spent all of their time getting business in the door, and workers provided all the effort, you would maximize profit. However, as mentioned above, partners are also workers. Clients expect the high expertise of partners to be applied to their work and, in fact, many make purchasing decisions with this in mind.

Another point to consider: partner work also generates revenue. In a situation where 25 percent of the work is performed by partners, about a third of the revenue comes from their time. The bottom-line is that work should be allocated to the right resources. Firms should make every effort to move the work down while ensuring that the timekeepers involved are constantly improving their skills and taking on higher levels of work.

A final important point on leverage: when it improves, the fees to clients go down. In other words, as work is pushed to lower-cost resources, the overall fee for a given piece of work should go down. We say "should" because this is dependent on the work being performed at competent lawyer levels. If work is pushed down to timekeepers who take too much time to complete tasks, the reasonable leverage line has been crossed. Staying on the right side of that line essentially means higher profits for firms and lower fees for clients. Truly the win-win result the market is begging for.

What you need to know about system components

Once you are grounded in basic firm economics, you need to gain an understanding of the basic components of matter coding, which will help you take knowledge management to a strategic level. When you combine your unique ability to leverage work product and know-how with an understanding of firm economics and matter coding, you'll be able to build processes and systems that help lawyers become more productive, firms more profitable, and clients more likely to come back to you. We will now introduce you to matter taxonomy, task codes, and templates. They're more interesting than they sound!

Matter taxonomy (aka collective experience)

Tracking matters, engagements, and people both internally and externally is essential to leveraging past work. Yet, until recently, most partners eschewed data at the detail level and focused on delivering the best legal work regardless of cost. Now, however, with customers applying pricing pressure, partners are scrambling to gather data that will help them analyze business opportunities, support proposal generation, and assign resources in a way that protects profitability. What they are finding is that much of the data collected during the new business intake process by admins is either inaccurate or incomplete. With the advent of legal process management, alternative fee arrangements, and matter budgeting tools, this is no longer acceptable. And here is where knowledge management professionals can step in and shine.

Strategically, a matter taxonomy gives the firm insight into business development, staffing matters, and where their profit comes from. Technology exists that will enable you to build out a matter taxonomy that allows the firm to tap into their collective experience. The challenge in the legal industry is that we do not have a cash register. In the world of retail, one person enters the critical information about a product, and every time the barcode passes the scanner, the data is captured. In the legal industry, we are dependent on people not scanners to capture the details for each matter.

In designing your taxonomy, you can capture a wide range of data. This includes core data – such as matter type, sub-type, area of law, client, and matter industry – to extended data that is dependent on the matter type or sub-type, including:

- Detail on the courts, judges, and vendors who participate in matters such as e-discovery for litigation and similar levels of detail for transactions; and
- Detail on the type of the transaction: what banks and accounting firms are involved and the size of the transaction.

The authors believe that in this approach you need to capture data in four big buckets: matter type, matter sub-type, area of law, and tags that provide additional description, such as the specific legal issues that are at stake. Key to streamlining the matter taxonomy build-out is to use technology that supports fields for multiple values, especially for tags. Multiple-value fields reduce the total number of columns required to describe matters, which streamlines the input process. Multiple-value fields are also very useful when no one category fits, such as when matters address more than one area of law.

Let's drill down now on the components of a matter taxonomy.

Matter type

Matter type is a very high-level description that groups the firm's work together into a *set* of particular processes, such as:

- *Transactions* – A set of processes where the output of the work is a contract or agreement of some kind;
- *Litigation* – An adversarial proceeding in front of a trier of facts (trial court, arbitration, hearing officer, etc.) or an appeals court;
- *Regulatory* – Working with a governmental agency to facilitate complying with a law or regulation;
- *Advisory* – Counseling the client on the risks related to certain business decisions;
- *Policy* – Lobbying on behalf of a client; and
- *Financial restructuring* – An unusually litigious process that combines both transactions and the bankruptcy process.

Matter sub-type

The matter sub-type is designed to describe the process itself rather than the subject area. In the US, the high-level process of suing in a trial court is the same no matter the venue or whether the matter involves malpractice, a contract dispute, or employment discrimination. Similarly, many regulatory processes are exactly the same. In these cases, the work can be simplified into several phases: fact gathering, drafting the form, client review, and filing. The goal here is to link the sub-type with a standard set of task codes or phases (more on this further on).

Standardizing the phases the firm uses to complete a particular type of work is advantageous in several ways in that it:

- Reduces the total number of possible phase codes used during time entry;
- Enables the comparison of phases across matters even when the subject area is different. This, in turn, enables effective pricing of matters across different subject areas; and
- Reduces the total number of selections presented to the user in the system.

Area of law

The "area of law" component of a matter taxonomy is intended to describe the legal subject area. This component of matter coding keeps the subject area relatively broad: for example, labor and employment, intellectual property, contract... Many times, the subject area may have the same name as the practice group. The area of law in the taxonomy will often require multiple values.

Tags

Tags are modifiers designed to provide additional detail as needed. As a general rule, tags will be filtered by the area-of-law selection. However, they may also be filtered by matter type or sub-type. For example, if "litigation" is selected as the matter type, "class action" may also be selected.

For each matter type, sub-type, and area of law, the practice group will need the ability to track additional fields. Here are two examples:

If the matter is litigation, you may want to track:

- Court;
- Judge;

- Demand;
- Outcome; and
- Completion phase.

If the matter addresses mergers and acquisitions, you may want to track:

- Industry of seller;
- Buy side or sell side; and
- Amount of acquisition.

Capturing the data

The matter-opening process is designed to determine whether the firm should take on the matter. Capturing this level of data during matter opening is not effective. Assistants fill out these forms, and they tend to pick the first data point on the list, or the one they use the most often. Assistants also often forget to ask for details.

A better approach is to create a process where data is captured throughout the life of the matter. The initial set of data should be collected about one week after matter opening and then on a scheduled basis, depending on the length of the matter. At a minimum, data should be collected twice: once in the beginning and once at the end of the matter. Critical data can often be gathered from other systems. For example, court data can be found in the docketing system.

Why capturing this data is important

Does this sound like too much work? Look at the payoffs listed below, and you'll better understand the strategic value of capturing this level of data:

- Allows the firm to make effective price searches to understand the effort and price associated with prior matters.
- Allows business development professionals to present the firm's collective experience in a pitch.
- Let's staff use similar matters as a starting point or precedent for new matters.
- Collects history – How many times has the firm has been in front of Judge X? How does he typically rule in a particular circumstance?

This information is valuable in pricing because it helps define scope and strategy. For example, if you can anticipate that Judge X always denies a motion to compel, you could decide not to file the motion, or you could reduce the scope of the work on these types of motions. Similarly, knowing that the judge will demand settlement before summary judgment will also signal how long the litigation will last.

- On the M&A front, when you are against firm X in a sell-side capacity, you can better forecast the key terms that will need to be negotiated and how long that typically takes.

Task codes

What's in a word? Lack of precision, often. The word "task" in the legal industry is often imprecisely used. Generally when we use it, the term "task" does not actually apply to a task in the traditional sense of the word, but to work performed during a phase or a sub-phase of a matter. Confused? Many of us are. Let's de-bunk the most common misuse of this terminology and get everyone on the same page.

The root problem dates back to the design of the ABA task codes and the Uniform Tasks Based Management System (UTMBS). The purpose of these coding systems was to enable electronic invoicing. This code set has been used primarily in the area of litigation and the cost codes around the management of expenses and disbursement.

Take the example of discovery in the ABA Litigation Code Set. The phase code for "discovery" is L300, which represents the discovery phase. The task codes include "written discovery", "document production", "depositions", "expert discovery", "discovery motions", and "other discovery". However, these labels all represent sub-phases, not tasks. The real tasks lie underneath.

Things got worse when many clients and law firms decided they didn't like the ABA labels and changed them to fit their needs. For example, the official label for L200 is "pre-trial pleadings and motions", but some clients want it to read "pleading and motions". As a result, within a single firm the same code can have slightly different meanings for different clients or for internal firm purposes.

The problem with all these codes is that a significant number of lawyers don't use them accurately. Anecdotally, we've been told on numerous occasions that as many as 60–80 percent of time entries have inaccurate codes. Much of the problem stems from the fact that there are over 29 codes in just the litigation code set. A choice of 29 codes is a lot, especially when you need to enter codes all of the time. If lawyers bill eight hours per day, they will need to make somewhere between eight and 20 time entries per day or 2,000 to 5,000 time entries per year. Whew!

Our general experience with look-up lists on frequents activities is that they should ideally number less than five entries and no more than 10. After 10, the accuracy of picking the correct selection diminishes pretty quickly. This conclusion is based on best practices that emerged from one of the author's experience designing and managing document management systems, which have exactly the same metadata problem.

While the UTMBS tasks codes are good for billing, they do not actually help you effectively price or estimate a matter. When you go back and look at a prior matter, you will find little information about critical details. In most US litigations, the critical details that make the difference in cost are the number of motions, number of documents, and number of depositions. This is next-to-impossible to ascertain because traditionally no one tracks the "real tasks" underneath the sub-phases.

To understand this better, let's turn back to the task labels that are really sub-phases, such as "document production", a sub-phase during which many specific tasks are carried out. Examples of these tasks include collecting documents, processing documents, planning for document review, reviewing documents, quality assurance regarding the reviews, and producing the documents. Some sub-phases are simpler but still problematic. For example, in the area of "depositions", you have two fundamental tasks: take a deposition and defend a deposition. These are very different things, but under e-billing they all get grouped under "depositions".

If you notice, all actual tasks start with a verb. Under each of these tasks are a multitude of activities that may be performed by different people. Let's take the example of taking a deposition:

- Schedule the deposition (secretary or paralegal);
- Pull the hot documents (associate);
- Review the documents (partner);
- Build an outline (partner);
- Take the deposition (partner); and
- Update the factual timeline (associate).

As you can see, we have three people involved in this one actual task, which means that process improvement may simply require improving the speed with which one of these activities gets done.

Measuring and getting to this level of detail is the nirvana. However, to get there, current technology is going to need to evolve, and the partners in your firm will need to agree on the list of tasks and activities in each phase and sub phase. Many practices have no task coding standard, especially for most of the transactional and regulatory matter types. Without coding standards, firms often struggle to get their practices better at pricing and delivering their services on budget. As a knowledge management professional, you can work with the partners and senior associates to establish a set of tasks codes for these matter sub-types. To do this, you will need to work with each practice group to define the phases and sub-phases of their work. The real struggle is always to balance the need for specificity with the reality of what people will actually enter in their time entries.

Templates

Pricing pressure pushes the need for templates and precedents. We live in a world where clients often will not pay for work they consider inefficient whether they are in an alternative fee arrangement or not. This creates an opportunity for you, as a knowledge management professional, to develop better templates that can be embedded into processes.

It is an easy sell: partners will recognize the efficiency of templates in terms of their impact on productivity, which we have learned is one of the factors that drive profit. Partners will also recognize the high cost of not readily finding information. Good access to information is the basis for improved decision making, it saves time and frustration, and it leads to less duplication of effort.

The value of integrating templates into your processes can be summarized in this way:

- Allows the firm to more easily push certain work down to less skilled associates, which reduces costs while improving leverage (another profit factor);
- Guides decision-making and enables legal professionals to work more effectively;
- Reduces seek time and the high cost of not readily finding information; and
- Makes appropriate documents available at the push of a button.

Netting it out

Law firms stuck in the past raise suspicions. Clients want firms that deliver high quality service at the right price. Please remember that high-paying, bet-your-business work is a perception of the client not the firm. More and more, legal services are perceived as a commodity, and clients are reluctant to sign up for services where fees cannot be projected and the work does not have to pass a litmus test.

As a result, non-standard fee arrangements have become the new normal. Non-standard arrangements come in a number of disguises, including very tight management of hourly rates and the billing process by the client. These factors all amount to the same thing: we can no longer count on profit being simply built in to the rate. Operational efficiency has become as important to law firms as growth to protect their profitability.

This chapter is a call to action for knowledge management professionals. In marketing terms, we call it increasing your brand. When you help the firm become more profit-driven by increasing operational efficiency at every level of the business, you are adding strategic value to a very high degree. And for this, your brand will morph from that of simply a resource to that of a change agent: one that helps your firm to continue to be profitable even as their market becomes very cost conscious.

Take a partner out to lunch. Describe how you visualize taking knowledge management to a strategic level. We bet the partner will pick up the bill.

Chapter 7: Componentized budgets for cost benefit analysis

By Bart Gabler, director of pricing and legal project management, K&L Gates, and Peter Lane Secor, director of strategic pricing and project management, Pepper Hamilton

Today, everyone is seeking the value proposition, trying to define and capture value. Warren Buffet's "price is what you pay and value is what you get" is one of the most basic and useful descriptions. How do you feel about what you paid for the service or item? Although value is driven by the end result or impact, componentized budgeting helps put a base value in perspective by using digestible chunks of value-added work. From front line attorneys to "C" level executives, everyone understands what is being done, what the cost of each item is, and why the prescribed activities are being performed. By calling out the specific building blocks of activities, clients are more empowered to make decisions that meet their business goals and objectives by weighing the costs/benefits of various activities of their legal services. Typically, the first pass at defining action items is done by the law firm although today with the greater sophistication of in-house legal departments we are seeing clients define their priorities around what needs to happen and when. Regardless of how the process starts, the end goal is a mutually agreed upon best practices cost efficient approach. This chapter explains what componentized pricing is; the methods to accomplish it, and how it can be used as a communications tool to communicate value to clients.

What is componentized pricing?

Think of componentized pricing from a cost accounting perspective: how many units of what, at what price, do we need to accomplish the end goal? We can do this for a divestiture, a purchase, a breach of contract, a class action, or any other legal service you can imagine. Typically, for legal services this is defined as hours and rates, often segregated by task codes. What the old standard, hours multiplied by rates, misses out on from a cost benefit analysis perspective are the real drivers of the costs of legal services: how many and what types of actions need to be done. It is the units, not the unit price, which drives cost.

For example: If we price five depositions at $20,000 each the total is $100,000. If we drop the unit price to $19,000 the total is $95,000, a 5 percent saving. However, if we drop to three depositions at the original price of $20,000 each the total is $60,000, a 40 percent saving.

Initiate activity	Unit fees	Units	Amount	Savings
Fact depositions Technicians	$20,000	5	$100,000	n/a
Fact depositions Technicians	$19,000	5	$95,000	5%
Fact depositions Technicians	$20,000	3	$60,000	**40%**

As pricing professionals, we cannot by any means recommend a specific approach from a substantive legal perspective but we can provide the breakdown of the underlying services in a format that allows our firm's lawyers and client GCs to discuss and make those determinations based on a variety of factors from risk mitigation, budget limitations, business objectives, timing, etc. By providing a budget with detailed tasks, componentized pricing enables increased client and law firm engagement around the key goals and objectives, and allows the client to really weigh-in on the trade-offs they are willing to make relative to cost vs value. It also helps align the interests and clarify the objectives at the onset of a matter, which improves efficiency and focus on the objectives that matter most to the client.

The components aren't always volume of units either; it could be the quality or type of unit. For example, in a corporate deal following due diligence, a law firm could layout options from a verbal summary, written bullet points of key findings to a memo describing each issue in detail. Each action is a product for the client and each action has both a value to the client and a cost of production. The goal with a componentized budget is to better engage the client in those discussions and to layout the tradeoffs for the client so they can determine what value makes the most sense to their organization.

There is much talk about the use of legal process outsourcing (LPO) which can be an effective strategy in reducing legal spend. But, again it is the number of units that really make the difference.

For example: If we have discovery for 12 custodians over five years the discovery fees could be in excess of a couple million dollars. However, if we can, through superior legal representation, reduce discovery to one custodian over three years it saves millions of dollars. The interesting part is that rate reductions do not have the same impact. It takes 10,000 hours to recognize $100,000 of savings from a $10 per hour decrease.

One of the goals for law firms is to help focus our client service around the tasks that drive the most value for the client. For example, within M&A, if we can leverage our experience to identify critical documents for review that are the most likely to be material for a "go vs no-go" decision, we can prioritize their review. The law firm can save the client both time and money, as well as better enable them to compete for the acquisition.

Componentized pricing can also be leveraged into relational pricing. Relational pricing is when you base one area of activities off another area of activities that is more predictable.

For example, attorneys can normally provide the number of days a trial will take, who will be on the trial team, and the anticipated hours per day. When viewed in isolation that information may not seem like much, but we can use that information to fairly accurately budget the anticipated costs of delivering that trial. If you are able to analyze various types of cases completed over the past couple years, you can even determine the percentage of work comparably for pre-trial efforts either based on task codes or just date ranges. For example, you could price the work based on units of days a trial runs; each day may not represent the same amount of work but you can determine an average for each day. This will align incentives on working towards a timely resolution and provide some price certainty on cost regardless of how much effort may be required (e.g., working nights or weekends).

Every matter has its variables – both known unknowns and unknown unknowns – so some can be anticipated in aggregate and others really cannot. The goal is to scope the budget to acknowledge that an unanticipated occurrence may require revisiting by the law firm and client. Variables that occur more frequently need to be accounted for establishing appropriate assumptions around the cost components in the budget. For example, you need to account for a difficult opposing counsel, additional complexity in reviewing documents, the number of times a draft is reviewed, etc. but you may not plan for fraud, complex environmental or tax issues, etc. For most law firms, they see enough work that they can look at certain types of matters as a portfolio; for one type of case pre-trial effort might be 150% of trial while others may represent small portion of the effort.

Here is an example of calculating the percentage of pretrial compared to trial:

Matter	A	B	C	D	E	F	Average
Trial fees	$150,000	$175,000	$250,000	$285,000	$315,000	$330,000	$250,833
Pre-trial fees	$195,000	$285,000	$360,000	$310,000	$414,000	$460,000	$337,333
Percentage	130%	162.9%	144%	108.8%	131.4%	139.4%	134.5%

By pricing in a componentized way for largely routine tasks, it allows for GCs to plan and anticipate costs. For example, for immigration matters, law firms can provide a per unit costs to complete certain tasks. The GC, in conjunction with their Human Resources Department, can evaluate their likely immigration legal needs and build an internal budget for their anticipated legal spend. Law firms also benefit in that it creates easy pricing, so removes any negotiation allowing law firms to be very responsive to opportunities, as well as enabling for easier cross-selling when colleagues can easily articulate the value proposition to their clients.

Immigration legal services	Per unit fee
1101 Preparation and filing of H-1B non-immigrant petition	XXXX
1102 Preparation and filing of amended H-1B petition	XXXX
1103 Preparation and filing of H-1B extension petition	XXXX
1109 Preparation and filing of H-4 dependents' petition	XXXX

1201 Preparation and filing of L-1 non-immigrant petition	XXXX
1202 Preparation and filing of amended L-1 petition	XXXX
1203 Preparation and filing of L-1 extension petition	XXXX

These methodologies or synergies can be easier to expose than one might think. Most firms and clients have tons of data, time entries available to develop unit costs and relationships. It is interesting though because each case is truly unique but in the end the 80/20 rule can apply. Much of what you learn can be applied to a broad spectrum of matters. Pricing professionals cannot do this alone – we need "matter" data to help us. The data can be obtained through cost driver/"matter management" databases, attorney interviews, analysis of narratives, review of matter plans, docketing, and more. Often, it's the combination of these approaches that is the most fruitful and helps balance different perspectives. Ultimately, the best lessons learned are by deploying a model that may err on the side of caution to start testing the market and collecting data.

Collecting componentized data

There are some extremely sophisticated matter management and data collections systems used by in-house legal departments and firms. The basis of this analysis starts with understanding the process and the component parts. Some firms have developed workflows to capture contextual or additional information about the matter. When the matter is opened and the type of engagement (labor, IP Lit, breach of contract, M&A, disposition, etc.) is defined and a specific workflow is assigned. The workflow will "check in" at predetermined times, based on the matter type, to get an update on the status of the engagement, or to collect other information such as: the amount at risk, success or failure on a motion to dismiss, the size of the document review, or a host of other cost drivers. Even a less sophisticated approach, like post matter debrief to articulate the size of the deal, outcome, financing terms, complexity, etc., can help provide similar information for developing componentized budget models. For instance you could work with a particular practice group to identify the drivers of costs including case length, jurisdiction, size of discovery, number of witnesses, number and types of motions, length of trial and more. No matter your approach or type of matter once you begin you'll be amazed at how much information you can collect, and how quickly. Start with a brief half hour meeting or meet individually with some attorneys and ask them what they think drives the length or complexity of a case (i.e., what will affect the cost to deliver the work). Compile it into a simple questionnaire, share and get buy-in, then start asking people to populate it with case information. Many of them can do it off the top of their heads. If not, other resources such as paralegals and litigation support can help. Now you can begin to compare matters. This case had six trial days and trial prep was $XXX, that case was a bench trial and post-trial spend was $XXX, the parallels you start to find will be astonishing. The information doesn't have to be perfect; trying to get to perfection is wasted time, it will evolve with time. Even the anomalies can be very helpful. When found ask what drove the anomalies, you might find a cost driver you hadn't considered or an efficiency gain that could be used in other situations. With this more macro information you can start to micro dig, looking at time entries and their narratives.

Once you understand the key activities, you need to codify that process. If you present that a deposition costs $XXX, you need to prescribe what is involved in the component of the budget in terms of estimated effort (i.e. hours) but more importantly in terms of what specifically the client receives. The hours are to provide a rough guideline on costs/effort involved and to minimize the risk of overrun but the goal is to be more granular for this activity (i.e., more closely connecting the hours to a specific outcome) and tying that work to something of value to the client.

Digging into the time entries and their narratives can be very intimidating. Most of us weren't involved in the engagements and there can be thousands or tens of thousands of rows depending on the size of the case. If you have started your matter management system/listing it is a great place to start. If you have not started a system a quick and easy method is to look at run rates. Make sure when you do this that you utilize the correct rate structure. Looking at spend on a matter five years old will not project out well for the upcoming years. You can start by looking at the hours involved (i.e., how much work was required to do the work) and who did the work by title/experience level. Or you can use a rate multiplier chart that converts old values to current values. Looking at rates and timekeepers can give you precise spend amounts but sometimes it can be hard and time consuming to match up the old timekeepers to new ones. The rate multiplier method adjusts rates to current values but not to specific timekeeper titles. In the end both methods provide current apples to apples values. Always remember to consider that today we have greater efficiencies and in some cases, lower cost alternatives, such as LPO or less expensive internal timekeepers.

Here is an example of what some of the data might look like when comparing run rates.

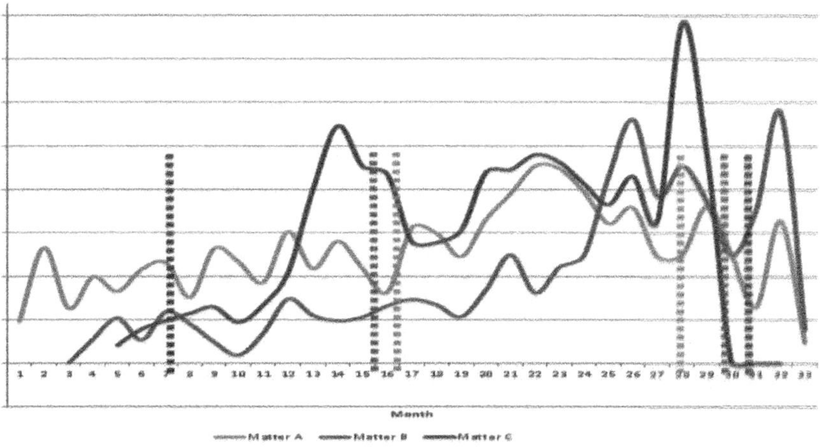

Figure 1: Comparing run rates

The lines are matter spends by month and the dotted lines represent the beginning and end of document discovery. What we couldn't understand from looking at the data was why the spend for Matter C, purple, was so much higher than the other matters. It turned out there were many delays on receiving the data and then a tremendous push at the end. While not the norm it was good for us to know what the spend could look like when there are extreme difficulties in obtaining discovery material. For "normal" discovery we could use the average run rates of Matter A and Matter B. The same methods can be used when comparing pre-trial and post-trial costs to trial costs. Not so tough, right? Don't forget to try and use a data set larger than three matters. You will indeed see similarities and learn from the non-conforming data. The next levels down are the component pieces, drilling down on the narratives.

Technology is working in our favor to help develop insight from the data law firms and clients have available. Matter planning, pricing and budgeting tools (e.g., BudgetManger, CAEL, Planning Blox, Iridium, Umbria, Cosine, and MatterWorks) are becoming key for many legal services providers; these tools provide quick analysis of matter performance and visual user interface to help engage both lawyers and clients in the matter performance review process. It also enables comparison of prior matters and the creation of budgets based on prior performance by key tasks. For example; you could find the amount for a motion for summary judgment for multiple matters. Unfortunately, most law firms do not yet have these technologies in place and we are forced to use other tools at our disposal, such as good old MS Excel.

L240 dispositive motions	**6/2/2017**	**$38,222**	**90.3**
Associate	6/2/2017	$322	1.4
Partner	5/4/2017	$19,470	35.4
Paralegal	5/4/2017	$541	0.2
Associate	6/2/2017	$18,389	53.3

Narrative Artificial Intelligence analysis is developing very quickly. Sky Analytics was one of the early vendors, however today there are a range of vendors either providing these services or offering software to help utilize the information. Many are focused on review invoice data provided to clients but more and more are turning to add law firms in assessing their time entry details. Some of vendors include Clocktimizer, Legal Decoder, Brightflag, and IBM Watson. These tools are developing rapidly and will help transform legal from looking at hours and rates to looking at the cost of various actions, in part because they will provide more structure to the available data. In addition, with experience these tools should also be able to provide context about what activities are being performed, as well as some level of prediction on when/why certain activities may occur (e.g. when dealing with a certain type of transaction or opposing council we typically see X iterations of a draft versus an average of Y firm wide). These insights will improve the ability to identify and price budget components, as well as better assess when certain components are necessary and at what cost.

Again, be careful to compare apples to apples ensure the value of your time entries is at current values. You can always adjust for discounting if needed. Drop the data in to Excel then using the "Search" function you can start to look at the cost of various activities.

For example: Here is how you might search to find out the cost of an oral argument.

Narrative	2015 STD	L530	Oral
Attend mock argument	$1,586	$1,586	
Review outline and Q/A	$396	$0	
Conference re oral argument preparation	$238	$238	$238
Attend argument	$1,427	$1,427	
=IFERROR(IF(SEARCH(AD$1,X48,1)>0,AB48,),"")			

If you have a matter planning/budgeting tool, you can drill into like matters and search for specific activities developed within the budget; alternatively, you can search by name, title, phase/task code, time range, narrative, practice, etc. This will enable relatively quick comparison of the work involved. Although these tools make it easier, they are not the only way to accomplish this task.

You can do the same for various motions, deponents, experts, witness, and more. Once you have created a column you can copy and paste to look for other key words or phrases. You do need to be careful. For example: motion for summary judgment could be listed as "MSJ", Summary Judgment, or any other variation. Once you find narratives that are on point, you may manually review proximal entries to gauge what others terms might be used to describe the activity. A couple of methods to ensure that narratives are consistent, which by the way can be important for client confidence in your time recording are: to provide memos by practice group or per engagement, to teach billers how entries should be phrased, and to periodically review time entries of ongoing matters. Additionally, you may review your Outside Counsel Guidelines which most likely have prescribed billing requirements.

Many people do not see the need for this level of analysis because they have task coding. The problem with straight task coding is that knowing the spend for a particular task code does not help firms or clients understand the actual costs per individual activity.

Here is an example:

Matter	Fees
Matter 00005	$65,394
Matter 00010	$95,329
Matter 00015	$174,366
Matter 00020	$91,704
Matter 00025	$115,987
Average	$108,556

Deponent	Fees
Deponent A	$25,086
Deponent B	$26,350
Deponent C	$27,487
Deponent D	$27,792
Deponent E	$25,149
Deponent F	$32,772
Average	$27,439

Figure 2: L330 – depositions

By just looking at L330 – depositions for various matters you have no idea what the individual costs are. The task code example on the left compared to the activity based example on the right clearly shows that the average cost per deposition is $27,500. A side benefit of this level of analysis is being able to identify run away depositions. As mentioned earlier this cannot be done in a vacuum if you are trying to determine the fees associated with a damages expert report – you will need to know the names of the experts for multiple matters. Be careful not to rely on the results of looking at one matter. With all this information, you can now accurately budget on a component basis.

Using componentized data

We have had to redact all the amounts from this sample budget. But, imagine now building a budget and asking targeted initial questions: will there be a motion to dismiss, will there be a motion for summary judgment, how many and what types of deponents do you envision, what kind of and how many experts to you anticipate, how long will the trial last, do you want to budget for the number of settlement days, and more. As you are working through this process you might hear an attorney say, "it is just my best guess." That's okay, and actually good.

This is just our starting point; very often a seasoned attorney's best guess is spot on but once on paper it's easier to engage other opinions or spot check with focused analysis.

Lead Partner:					
Initiative	**Unit Fees [2]**	**Units**	**Amount [2]**	**Percentage Complete**	**Amount Complete**
Analysis, Strategy, Communications, *Fact Development, and Investigation, Project Management*		*X%*	$XXX	*X%*	$XXX
Motions					
Motion to Dismiss	$XXX	*X*	$XXX	*X%*	$XXX
Motion to Transfer Venue(possible)	$XXX	*X*	$XXX	*X%*	$XXX
Written Discovery	$XXX	*X*	$XXX	*X%*	$XXX
Document Review (Est. X Terabytes reduced X%)	$XXX	*X*	$XXX	*X%*	$XXX
Discovery Disputes	$XXX	*X*	$XXX	*X%*	$XXX
Fact Depositions					
Client	$XXX	*X*	$XXX	*X%*	$XXX
Plaintiff	$XXX	*X*	$XXX	*X%*	$XXX
Technicians	$XXX	*X*	$XXX	*X%*	$XXX
Expert Discovery					
Client Industry Experts					
Selection	$XXX	*X*	$XXX	*X%*	$XXX
Reports	$XXX	*X*	$XXX	*X%*	$XXX
Deposition	$XXX	*X*	$XXX	*X%*	$XXX
Plaintiff's Experts					
Depositions	$XXX	*X*	$XXX	*X%*	$XXX
Motion for Summary Judgment	$XXX	*X*	$XXX	*X%*	$XXX
Settlement Activity / Mediation (days)	$XXX	*X*	$XXX	*X%*	$XXX
Trial Prep (X% of trial)		*X%*	$XXX	*X%*	$XXX
Trial (Days)	$XXX	*X*	$XXX	*X%*	$XXX
Post Trial (Bench X% of prep and trial)		*X%*	$XXX	*X%*	$XXX
TOTAL FEES			$XXX		$XXX

Figure 3: Sample litigation template

Here is the great part about this, when attorneys sit down to review and revise, they aren't thinking about rates and hours, they are thinking about what it takes to accomplish the desired results. Do we really think the doc review size will be that large or that complicated? Of course, you can apply the same methods to transactions; what areas of due diligence are needed, can we waive some to decrease the spend? Now we are talking about the overall approach and calibrating to the likely cost of the components, as well as evaluating risk management and attorneys can help make sure that there are no surprises. Pricing and procurement are still part of the discussion, but the roles are about supporting the unit costing rather than the overall budget. Be careful, in the procurement world cost saving is different than cost avoidance. Some of this might be considered cost avoidance; do we really need to have this expert? But, in the end it is the talent of the lawyers that enable these decisions to be made.

Additionally, a componentized budget is an effective tool for discussing the overall fee arrangement. Too often law firms and clients engage in a price discounting negotiation, which may result in lower fees for the client but may not address their exact needs in terms of value. Instead, the goal with a componentized budget is to focus on the activities that will best meet the desired outcome and the desired price, ultimately resulting in value to the client.

Unfortunately, this process is really only the beginning of matter management. Now the budget must be managed and everyone must be kept informed. One method shown on the example above is percentage based accounting. It works. Percentage based accounting is traditionally used in construction with payments based on the portion of work completed. It is very easy for a senior associate on a team to provide monthly updates on what activities are complete or partially complete. It also provides a level of accountability for the team staffed on the matter by giving and a sense of what the expectations are. If you have done everything right your matter run rates will be very close to what has actually been accomplished. But, there will be exceptions. It might be an issue that the law firm can manage internally (e.g., wrong staffing mix, breakdown in the workflow, quality control); these can be reviewed by the partner and addressed prior to a major issue arising. However, any issues require discussions with the client because they might impact the expected delivery of legal services in that it could cause delay, require additional services/units, or the risk assessment may have changed necessitating a chance in approach. Typically, a quick conversation with the team will reveal what is happening. By building out a componentized budget tool it provides a mechanism for easy assessment by the client service team, from monthly or weekly progress check-ins to a quick update call from a project manager. If your team is running effectively and providing your client with good communications everyone will already be aware of any situations and likely be in a position to engage both partners and clients in advance of any issues. Some external drivers that can be of impact are overly contentious opposing counsel, large expert reports, additional unanticipated motions, and change of client strategy.

The key is where to start. If you look at the whole firm, it may seem overwhelming and difficult to get your arms effectively around the data. Perhaps focusing on a practice area or a particular matter type can help to both focus your efforts as well as build your substantive knowledge of the work type. However, you need attorneys and paralegals that have an appetite to engage, and ideally a client willing to do the same. You need on-going feedback to develop and refine this approach. Much like Rome, it wasn't built in a day – but even a simple componentized cost model can yield fruit in the form of budgets and approaches that client's view as valuable to delivering the results they deserve and expect from their outside counsel.

Budgeting is a learning tool, every time we do one we get better at it.

Chapter 8: Creating a realistic matter budget

Sally Dyson, director, Firm Sense Ltd

"Can you honestly think of any other purchase decision that is made on the basis of an uncertain outcome, an uncertain price, and an uncertain incidence of when the price has to be paid?" – Paul Gilbert

Are budgets necessary?

Many lawyers have not traditionally felt the need to create a matter budget before commencing work on a matter. As Paul Gilbert has noted in his book *Head2Head*, until recently, law firms could "get away with answering the question of 'what will it cost?' with a well-practised sorrowful shrug and a trust-me look".[1]

This approach will rarely wash with clients these days. Even those prepared to pay on the basis of hourly rates increasingly demand to know the likely fee quantum in advance. In this way they can make an informed decision on whether to proceed with a matter, and ensure that they will only be incurring legal fees that they can afford to pay. Again, Paul Gilbert is instructive here when he says, "Can you honestly think of any other purchase decision that is made on the basis of an uncertain outcome, an uncertain price, and an uncertain incidence of when the price has to be paid?"

Certain types of more commoditized legal work have a recognized market price. This might apply to residential conveyancing or drawing up a will. Complex, bespoke transactions do not. Despite solicitors in England and Wales being bound by Code of Conduct requirements, which specify that "you must give your client the best information possible about the likely overall cost of a matter both at the outset and, where appropriate, as the matter progresses,"[2] lawyers have too readily assumed that it is impossible to predict a matter's likely cost when in fact they have often not made any robust attempt to do so.

There is no denying that time and effort is required for a lawyer to produce a reliable cost estimate. Lawyers may have considered that time spent planning a matter was wasted or non-recoverable time. Additionally, the skills required tend not to be taught at law school and as a result, lawyers have felt absolved from the responsibility of accurately predicting a matter's likely cost. This approach is misguided for the following reasons:

- Clients are increasingly refusing to bear all the risk of the cost of a matter and are requiring their firms to offer fixed, capped or value fees. They are also abandoning firms that cannot offer AFAs in favor of firms that can;
- Firms that do offer AFAs must understand what their costs are likely to be or they will not be able to operate AFAs profitably; and
- Firms must understand their costs before agreeing to any rate or fee discounts, or they may find themselves working at a loss, which in the long term becomes unsustainable.

At a minimum, a matter budget will provide the following vital pieces of information:

- The cost to the firm of conducting the matter;
- The fee to be charged to the client; and
- The profit amount and profit margin in percentage terms that will achieved by the firm at the price set.

This chapter will demonstrate how it is possible, even on the most complex matters, to create reasonably accurate matter budgets that will satisfy clients. It will examine the information that a lawyer needs to have available and will provide simple tools which will enable the lawyer to organize and process the relevant data. In turn, this will enable them to calculate both the cost to the firm and the range of possible fees which could be charged to the client. The actual fee that the firm will finally charge will depend on the strength of the relationship and the ability of the lawyer to negotiate the fee.

As a sample transaction, this chapter uses an imagined purchase of shares of an imagined private company (Hypothetical UK LLP) in order to illustrate the mechanics of creating a matter budget. Accounts for Hypothetical UK LLP are provided in Table 1, and further data needed to create the matter budget is supplied in Table 3 of this chapter.

The link between annual and matter budgets

Law firm budgets have become ubiquitous. It would be rare indeed to find a firm these days which had not set a firm-wide budget for the next 12 months, and most likely for a longer period of around three years.

Personal budget targets are also highly pervasive. A majority of firms set billable hours targets for their fee earners. A more enlightened approach sees law firms introducing billing targets which reflect fees earned rather than hours recorded. Lawyers will need to consider their firm and personal targets, and the number of matters that they are likely to complete in the course of a year when setting their prices. If the firm's leadership is transparent with its lawyers and other fee earners, then they are likely to know the expected profit margin that the firm either aims to achieve as a whole or, more usefully, that the firm leadership expects from their particular practice area.

When pricing a matter, the lawyer needs to be mindful of the profit margin that they are expected to deliver on each matter. There will be occasions when a deviation from expected matter profitability can be acceptable in the interests of securing a new client or developing a new relationship which has a lot of potential. But once a client has become accustomed to working with a law firm at a particular price point, it will be hard to justify raising fees if there is not a commensurate increase in the quality of work or the value provided to the client. In this way, loss leaders all too often translate to losses.

There is not much benefit to the firm of fee earners keeping themselves busy with lots of low margin work (except in volume businesses where this is firm strategy). Personal and firm budgets can guide a lawyer towards the ball park in which fees need to be set if targets are to be met. The amount that the fee earner will be able to charge will of course depend on what the matter is worth to the client and what is considered a reasonable fee for the work to be done. This is the (multi) million-dollar question that lawyers struggle with. To answer it, lawyers should deploy historic matter information, matter plans and matter budgets, all of which are explained in this chapter.

Historic price information

While no two matters will be identical, law firms are sitting on a mine of historic matter information, which they would be well advised to take advantage of. They are also constantly generating fresh intelligence to be added to the databank. This information is held both at the individual and institutional level but is not always captured or analyzed sufficiently. It is useful for both for the lawyers to review their own files, and for the firm to carry out retrospective studies for different, common transaction types.

Some lawyers work on a much higher volume of matters than others and some matters take many months to complete. Many transactions will not complete. This means that there is no right answer as to how many transactions a lawyer should analyze in order to create a credible fee range. There is also no correct response as to how far back in time a lawyer should delve. Much will depend on global and local economic factors as well as the trends in the legal market. In the teeth of a recession, there is little point at looking back at fees charged prior to the downturn. As a rule of thumb, it is probably best to concentrate on the previous two or three years only. This may not produce a wealth of data for an individual lawyer. There will be a much greater volume of data if all similar transactions conducted by the firm or practice group are amalgamated. It will also be very instructive for the lawyer to obtain information about the charging habits of other lawyers in the group. The large variations between the fees charged by members of a team can often be accounted for by working practices, confidence and negotiation skills, rather than absolute worth of a matter. Practice group heads and individuals can take action to improve their revenue generation in the light of information obtained by a group survey.

As law firm time recording systems were mainly established for the purposes of generating invoices rather than to support budgeting activity, firms may not be able to obtain the level of granularity that they would like from their firm-wide historic matter information. They should seriously consider the possibility of upgrading their systems for this purpose. In the US, for example, many law firms are now adopting a 'phase and task' approach to time recording, based upon the American Bar Association (ABA)'s billing codes[3]. Pending firm-wide system development, lawyers can at least use their own memories and examine their own files to provide the nuances – the reasons why one transaction was more expensive than another, which they may not yet be able to derive from firm-wide data.

By looking back over invoices delivered to past clients for similar matters, lawyers can see if patterns and price ranges emerge. Lawyers will need to bear in mind that there are a range of factors which may have influenced the fee that was charged. A list of the key variables which could impact a purchase of a private company is set out below:

- Urgency;
- Value to the client;

- Complexity – for example, multiple jurisdictions, risks within the target or structuring;
- Cooperativeness or hostility of the target, sellers and their advisers;
- Employee issues;
- Regulatory issues;
- Economic conditions affecting the client's ability or willingness to pay and the law firm's need to take on work;
- How the work was won – for example, competitive e-auctions will drive down price;
- The attitude of the client both to working with the law firm and to paying fees;
- The skill and experience of the client;
- The negotiating ability of the lawyer;
- The skill of the lawyer's team assigned to the matter;
- The extent to which the lawyer managed and guided the team;
- Cooperativeness of the client's other advisers – for example, bankers and accountants; and
- Whether the transaction completed or aborted.

Most of these variables will be at play in any corporate transaction. There will be a similar list affecting other transaction types. It is helpful to make a note of any key variables which unduly skewed the final outcome in each transaction.

When pricing a matter, the better the lawyer knows the client and the client's business, the easier it is for the lawyer to predict how easy or difficult the transaction will be and to adjust the price accordingly. If the lawyer had handled similar transactions in the past for the particular client, the lawyer can compare the fees charged to that client with the fees charged for the client group as a whole and make allowances accordingly in the price proposal.

Matter plans

Historic matter information provides the big picture view of the likely overall fee range but this range is still likely to be too wide. Particularly in complex and bespoke matters, the lawyer will need to create a much more detailed matter plan, which shows each anticipated step in the transaction or case and allocates resource and time to completing each step. Not only will the process of creating a matter plan significantly improve the accuracy of any fee estimate, it will also enable the lawyer to estimate the time required to complete the matter; to build the most appropriate team; and, once the matter has progressed, to track performance against plan. To manage a matter, a lawyer needs to have some expectations against which to manage, whether it is achieving a milestone on time or on budget. If the matter starts to go off track for any reason, the lawyer will be able to make adjustments to the team and their priorities or consult with the client before an overrun becomes an issue.

In order to create a matter budget, the lawyer will need to have considered the tasks to be performed, the skill level required to conduct each task, the available staff and the likely time each task will take. Only by pulling all this information together will the lawyer begin to develop a more accurate picture of the cost to the firm of conducting the matter and the appropriate fee to charge.

Firms should be encouraged to create matter templates for all common transaction types they undertake. If this is not done at firm level, the lawyer can create matter templates for the matter types undertaken by that lawyer. Although data which is more than three years old would need to be treated with great caution in setting a matter price, the tasks required to be undertaken in order to complete any given matter type are likely to have remained static for a much longer period. Therefore, in creating matter templates, lawyers can have recourse to older historic records. A sample matter template for the purchase of a private company is provided at Appendix 1. Alternatively, lawyers may choose to adopt the ABA's Uniform Task-Based Management System referred to above.

The lawyer should create a matter plan for every new matter. The process will be quickest if the lawyer is able to base the matter plan on an existing matter template but the matter plan can be created from scratch if necessary. A summary extract from a matter plan for a purchase of a private company is set out in Table 2. Each major phase of the transaction is described and a number of hours of fee earner time is allocated to each phase. The matter plan specifies how much time should be spent by partners, assistant solicitors and trainees. The information has been condensed here but in reality, each phase should be broken down into its constituent parts as shown in the more detailed matter template in Appendix 1.

The matter plan represents the best guess of the lawyer as to the amount of time that each fee earner will need to spend on each stage of a matter. It is unlikely to be 100 percent accurate. It can be helpful

Balance sheet		
Fixed assets	£30,000,000	
Current assets		
Debtors & WIP on accruals basis	£80,000,000	
Cash	£5,000,000	
Amounts due from members	£15,000,000	
	£100,000,000	
Current liabilities		
Bank overdraft	£15,000,000	
Loans	£10,000,000	
Creditors	£5,000,000	
Tax	£10,000,000	
Accruals	£10,000,000	
	£50,000,000	
Net current assets (current assets less current liabilities)		£50,000,000
Net assets attributable to members (total assets less current liabilities)		£80,000,000
Represented by:		
Loans & other debts due to members		£20,000,000
Equity		£60,000,000
		£80,000,000
Total members interests		
Amounts due from members		-£15,000,000
Loans due to members		£20,000,000
Equity		£60,000,000
		£65,000,000

Profit and loss account	
Income	£200,000,000
Staff costs	-£70,000,000
other expenses	-£65,000,000
Operating profit	£65,000,000
Net interest payable/receivable	-£500,000
Profit before members' remuneration	£64,500,000
Members' remuneration	£14,500,000
Net profit	£40,000,000

Key metrics	
Operating profit margin	32.5%
Total no. partners	180
Equity partners	100
Salaried partners	80
Members' remuneration	£14,500,000
Net profit for distribution to Equity Partners	£40,000,000
Profit per equity partner	£400,000
Gearing	1:5
Debtors & WIP in months	5

Table 1: Hypothetical UK LLP – simplified accounts and key metrics

to create best-case and worst-case scenario matter plans. The actual amount of time that will be taken is likely to be somewhere between the two.

Task	Details	Chargeable hours by fee earner type				Sub total
		Partner	Senior assistant	Junior assistant	Trainee	
1	Initiating discussions and establishing relationships	10	17	8		35
2	Due diligence	12	15	150	195	372
3	Structuring	12	15	40		67
4	Sale documentation	80	240	150	80	550
5	Completion documentation	4	2	30	8	44
6	Regulatory advice and clearances	8	40		20	68
7	Funding arrangements	40	60	60	35	195
8	Post-completion matters			6	20	26
9	Co-ordination	35	40	50	25	150
	Totals	**156**	**372**	**436**	**383**	**1,472**

Table 2: Extract from a matter plan for the purchase of a private company

The best guess will not be wild or uneducated if the lawyer has already followed the advice given above on the use of historic matter information, to provide a realistic basis for the number of hours to be spent. As also mentioned above, the better the lawyer knows the client then the more accurate the matter plan will be. Similarly, the better the lawyer responsible for drawing up the matter plan is acquainted with the deal team and the more they have worked together, the more finely honed the hours estimate will be.

Matter budgets

In order to calculate the fee that can be charged to the client for a matter, the high-level outputs of the matter plan need to be fed into a matter budgeting tool. The matter budget is a form of financial model designed to enable lawyers to price their work. At its most basic, the matter budget shows:

- The rates that each fee earner charges;
- The number of hours that each fee earner is expected to work on each of the key tasks to be performed on the matter (with the numbers drawn directly from the matter plan);
- The expected margin that the firm will achieve; and
- Any variance between budget and actual figures.

The lawyer should be encouraged to stress test the model to show what will happen to the profit margin if the number of hours worked is increased while the fee remains static, or if the fee is discounted. It can be quite shocking for a lawyer to see the impact of a ten percent fee discount on the firm's bottom line.

Table 3 sets out basic information about Hypothetical UK LLP, which will be needed to create a matter budget. Table 4 shows the matter budget for the company acquisition on which Hypothetical UK LLP has been instructed. An explanation of the underlying calculations and a glossary of financial terms is provided at Table 5, while a blank matter budget calculator is set out at Appendix 2. The matter budget can be adjusted by lawyers to meet their needs. If the fee seems too high or the margin too low then the lawyer has the opportunity to adjust the matter plan and matter budget before work on the matter commences. For example, the number of hours of partner time may need to be reduced in favor of more hours undertaken by a senior assistant to deliver the target profit margin. In the short term, if the lawyer realizes that the matter cannot reasonably be contained within the fee that the client is prepared to pay, then the lawyer can talk openly with the client about how the matter could be managed differently in order to make it more economic. The client may agree that the timetable can be lengthened, or that they will take on more of the administrative aspects of managing the matter. The crucial point is that the lawyer is armed with the necessary information before work on a matter commences. And by conducting an informed discussion with the client before any costs have been incurred, the lawyer is likely to arrive at a mutually agreeable position which meets the client's needs yet is affordable and delivers the appropriate profit to the firm.

Hourly rates

	Standard rate
Partner	£500
Senior assistant	£400
Newly qualified	£200
Trainee	£100

Hours targets

Partner	1,500
Assistant	1,800
Trainee	1,000

Staff costs

	Net salary	Tax, social security, pensions	Total salary
Equity Partner notional salary	£400,000		£400,000
Senior Assistant	£100,000	25,000	£125,000
Newly qualified	£60,000	15,000	£75,000
Trainee	£30,000	7,500	£37,500

Margins

	Cost per hour (annual total salary / billable hours)	Gross margin per hour on standard rates (standard rate less cost per hour)	Gross % profit margin on standard rates (margin / fee x 100)
Equity Partner	£267	£233	47%
Senior Assistant	£69	£331	83%
Newly qualified	£42	£158	79%
Trainee	£38	£63	63%

Table 3: Hypothetical UK LLP – Budget components

Hourly statistics					
	Partner	Snr Asst	Jnr Asst	Trainee	
Standard rate	£500	£400	£200	£100	
Recovered rate @ 80%	£400	£320	£160	£80	
Hourly salary cost	£267	£69	£42	£38	
Margin	£233	£331	£158	£62	

Matter plan					
	Chargeable hours by fee earner type				
Details	Partner	Snr Asst	Jnr Asst	Trainee	Sub total
Initiating discussions and establishing relationships	10	17	8		35
Due diligence	12	15	150	195	372
Structuring	12	15	40		67
Sale documentation	80	240	150	80	550
Completion documentation	4	2	30	8	44
Regulatory advice and clearances	8	40		20	68
Funding arrangements	40	60	60	35	195
Post completion matters			6	20	26
Co-ordination	35	40	50	25	150
Totals	**156**	**372**	**436**	**383**	**1,472**

Matter total fees					
	Partner	Snr Asst	Jnr Asst	Trainee	Total
Standard fees	£78,000	£148,800	£87,200	£38,300	£352,300
Recovered fees	£62,400	£119,040	£69,760	£30,640	£281,840
Salary cost	£41,652	£25,668	£18,312	£14,554	£100,186

Matter margins			
	Benchmark	Recovered	Variance
Fees	£352,300	£281,840	£70,460
Salary cost	£100,186	£100,186	
Gross margin	£252,114	£181,654	
Gross margin %	72%	64%	
Other overhead	£114,498	£114,498	
Operating profit	£137,617	£67,157	51%
Operating profit margin %	39%	24%	

Table 4: Hypothetical UK LLP – Simplified matter budget for the purchase of a private company

Adapted from materials provided by Robert Mowbray of Taylor Mowbray LLP, with thanks

Term	Explanation	Example
Salary costs per hour	Salary cost of the individual divided by that individual's billable hours targets	£125,000 = £69 1,800 hours
Other overhead	Non salary costs	Usually a separate line item in the profit and loss account
Other overhead percentage	Figure for other overhead divided by turnover and then multiplied by 100	£65,000,000 x100 = 32.5% £200,000,000
Other overhead per matter	Matter revenue at standard hourly rates multiplied by the other overhead percentage	£352,300 x 0.325 = £114,498
Gross margin per hour	The individual's hourly rate less the individual's salary costs per hour	£400 - £69 = £331
Gross margin percentage on hourly rates	Gross margin per hour divided by the hourly rate multiplied by 100	£331 x 100 = 83% £400
Gross margin percentage on overall fee	Gross margin on matter fee divided by matter fee and multiplied by 100	£252,114x 100= 72% £352,300
Operating profit	Fees less salary costs and other overhead	£352,300 – (£100,186+£114,498) = £137,617
Operating profit margin percentage	Operating profit divided by the fee and then multiplied by 100	£137,617x100 = 39% £352,300
Net profit	Operating profit plus or minus interest receivable or payable less members' remuneration	(£65,000,000 - £500,000) - £14,500,000 = £40,000,000
Profit per equity partner	Net profit of the firm divided by the number of equity partners	£40,000,000 100 =£400,000 per partner
Recovered rate per hour	The standard hourly rate multiplied by the percentage recoverable. So if a 20 percent discount is given, the percentage recoverable is 80 percent.	£400 x 0.8 = £320
Gearing	The number of salaried fee earners for every equity partner, expressed as a ratio	If there are 100 equity partners and 500 salaried fee earners the gearing is 1:5
Lock-up	The time, often expressed in days, between starting work on a matter and getting paid. It comprises work in progress which is work performed but not yet billed and debtors which is work billed but not yet paid	If it takes a firm on average 80 days to issue a bill after opening a matter and a further 70 days to get paid then the lock-up will be 80+70 = 150 days

Table 5: A glossary and guide to law firm financial calculations

In the longer term, matter budgets will deliver insights which can inform the firm's business model and strategy. The firm may reach the conclusion that matter processes need a wholesale overhaul in order to be conducted profitably at prices that clients will bear. It may need to encourage colleagues to share precedents in order to avoid reinventing the wheel on each matter and it may become apparent that it is worthwhile or even necessary for the firm to invest in technological solutions, such as automated document assembly, in order to cut costs. The firm may choose to focus their business development efforts on those matters which deliver the greatest level of returns and may decide to withdraw from providing lower margin services. The need to make such decisions is likely to come to light much sooner where firms are forced to consider the profitability of each matter as they create and manage matters to matter budgets. Decisions will be more rational and defensible as a result of being data driven.

A word on tools

The sample matter templates, matter plans and budget calculators used in this chapter have all been created very simply using Excel. For lawyers working individually without wider firm support, an Excel spreadsheet is all that is required to create perfectly functional tools. Excel has the advantage of being built into every lawyer's computer and the basics can be mastered very quickly. For these reasons, some firms will choose to roll out firm-wide tools which also rely on Excel.

Other firms will prefer to invest in more specialized technology. There are several off-the- shelf products designed with law firm budget creation in mind, from providers such as Aderant and Thomson Reuters. However, these tools tend to require a level of user expertise not yet pervasive in law firms. It is likely that such tools will continue to be refined in the coming years. Meanwhile, firms may elect to design software specifically tailored to their needs. Whichever solution is chosen, the firm needs to ensure that its fee earners:

- Appreciate and accept the value to them and to the firm of preparing matter budgets;
- Understand the benefits to them and to the firm of using the tools;
- Are fully trained on the use of the tools; and
- Find the tools simple and intuitive to use.

If these criteria are not met, firms will find that the budgeting tools are neglected and their lawyers continue either to avoid providing fee estimates or regularly underestimate the cost to the firm of conducting a matter, leading to lower than forecast profits or even losses.

This chapter has shown that in an era of increased client activism, few firms can afford to continue to launch directly into working on a matter without first creating a matter budget. In order to create a matter budget, lawyers should bear in mind annual firm and personal targets and strategies and should make use of any historic matter information available to them. All this intelligence should be fed into a matter plan which itself will be a component in the matter budget. The matter budget can be used to determine the way that the matter should be resourced, the time it should take to complete and the optimal price to be achieved by the law firm. By manipulating the figures in the matter budget, the lawyer can create a number of pricing options to present to the client in negotiations. The matter budget will also be an essential tool which the lawyer can rely on to manage the matter effectively. Many lawyers will have had no prior experience of pricing their matters in this way and will need extensive training and coaching to develop their competence and confidence in the new ways of working.

References

1. Gilbert, P., 2002. *Head2Head*, Author Publishing Ltd: Suffolk
2. Solicitors Regulation Authority, Solicitors Code of Conduct 2007, Rule 2.03, http://www.sra.org.uk
3. American Bar Association, Uniform Task-Based Management System, http://www.americanbar.org

Chapter 9: Managing client intake to increase profitability

By Anthony E. Davis, partner, Hinshaw & Culbertson LLP, and Wendy Wen Yun Chang, partner, Hinshaw & Culbertson LLP

In the wake of the Great Recession, the legal profession has seen a fundamental and permanent change. Today, to be successful, a law firm must operate as a business while continuing to provide quality legal services. The statistics and various reports from legal services industry commentators point to the same conclusion: the total spend by corporate buyers of legal services from traditional law firms remains flat, while those same buyers simultaneously demand law firm efficiencies. Clients want more work done at a lower total cost. Unless firms adapt, this translates to smaller profit margins – or losses. In this changed world, effective client intake management is a critical tool for firms to employ in furtherance of remaining both competitive and profitable.

Client selection

Every lawyer and law firm goes through times where economic considerations appear to favor taking any client and matter that walks in the door, on the theory that any work is better than no work. In the short term, this approach may even *feel* better, because there is work to do, leading to a false belief that profitability merely depends on the existence of work. This is not true. Profitability depends on lawyers being paid for their work at a rate that exceeds their costs of doing the work. To attain profitability, sometimes it is better not to take on every prospective client, because not every client is a good client. The best risk and client intake management systems effectively match the *right* clients for the firm and its lawyers – and identify the likely unprofitable engagements so that they can be rejected.

Properly evaluating conflicts

The duty of loyalty is at the core of the attorney-client relationship. Failure to identify conflicts quintessentially violates that duty and can lead to costly and hard to defend claims of malpractice, breach of fiduciary duty, disgorgement of fees, disqualification, and even professional discipline.

Identifying conflicts of interest are therefore the first step of every client intake decision, and every law firm has some form of conflicts analysis system. For some firms, the process is manual, where lawyers circulate the name of prospective clients amongst all attorneys in the firm, and every lawyer is required to review the information, which necessarily takes up a significant amount of attorney time. Further, because this type of manual system relies on fallible human memory, as well as a good understanding on everyone's part of the ethics rules governing conflicts, it is prone to error.

A significant proportion of malpractice claims allege both a legal error and a conflict of interest, which could, and should, have been caught and addressed during the intake process. Lawyers eager to start work ignore believing that there will never be a problem, or that they will be able to "handle" it if one arises. At the beginning of an attorney client relationship, clients are happy and the relationship is fresh. Lawyers do not think at that stage about how that relationship may sour and about the consequences if it does. A conflict that should have been addressed up front can create liability that may be independent of any claimed error. Clients routinely argue they would not have engaged the law firm had they known of the conflict. Cases where conflicts are alleged are hard to defend. Juries find them troubling, and are unforgiving. The consequences for the firm can be quite severe – liability, disgorgement of fees, damage to the firm's reputation, and potentially even professional discipline.

Laterally hired lawyers are a special risk category for firms, with particular reference to conflicts of interest. New lawyers may not be used to a rigorous intake review process, and may try to bypass it whenever they can. Strong intake systems need to be set up to make ignoring the firm's intake protocol very difficult, if not impossible. Firms should pay careful attention to lateral compliance with firm intake processes and take steps to enforce compliance from the moment lawyers join the firm.

Many firms are moving toward using automated conflicts checking software tools, where a prospective client's name is run against a database of a firm's current and former clients, identifying which lawyer handled which matter at what particular point in time, as well as names of other parties involved in the matter. A conflicts report is then generated which is reviewed either by the attorney seeking to open a new file or, more efficiently, by professional conflicts staff who are generally supervised by the office of general counsel. The analysts are trained to identify and understand conflicts, and in many instances, they do understand more about the subject than most lawyers. Under the supervision of a lawyer, non-lawyer analysts can be a cost-effective way of handling the conflict review process, as the analysts can process the vast majority of the conflicts inquiries, and only escalate the complex conflicts questions to the attorney seeking to open the file, and, when needed, to the firm's general counsel. This system minimizes the time necessary for attorneys to devote to the process, freeing them up to work on billable client matters – knowing they can do so free of the risks of conflicts of interest. For these reasons, these systems are more accurate, more comprehensive and much more likely to enable firms to comply with the ethics rules.

Even when the checking is done using purpose built software, in firms where the file opening lawyer is the one required to perform the conflicts analysis from the report generated by the software, it also suffers from the drawbacks that non-billable attorney time is wasted, and the critical element of independent review based on an understanding of the conflicts rules is missing.

Evaluating prospective clients for financial suitability

Historically, financial analysis of prospective clients for financial suitability, independent of the lawyer seeking to introduce the business, has not usually been a part of intake management. Law firm general counsel have not traditionally seen this as part of their responsibilities, even though they see the effects of the acceptance of unsuitable clients at the end point. But when confronted with problems associated with collections, general counsel often do wonder why the firm accepted the client in the first instance. These end point problems can be substantial, presenting ethical, legal, and financial problems. As a predicate matter, permissive withdrawals can only be effectuated if there will be no material adverse effect on the interests of the client, and after the firm has taken steps to avoid reasonably foreseeable adverse consequences to a client before that withdrawal. This may mean, in some circumstances, being ethically required to continue to provide legal services even if the client owes the lawyer substantial fees and there is little prospect of the firm getting paid. In litigation, court permission is required to withdraw, and courts may not approve the request especially if the firm waits too long to ask, leaving the firm obligated to perform legal services competently, again with no prospect of getting paid. In these situations, large accounts receivable just get bigger. Suing a client for fees is often not a viable option and is always likely to draw a cross-complaint for legal malpractice. Clients who cannot pay a firm in the first place are unlikely to be able to satisfy a judgment for fees even if the firm obtains one.

Despite these problems, firms all too often fail to draw the connection between managing the risks of bad end point consequences and making informed decisions about client selection on the front end. When general counsel try to impose financial evaluation standards on prospective clients at the front end, they face resistance from the firm's lawyers. Whoever is assigned the task of evaluating the suitability and potential profitability of prospective engagements, firms need to assign this role in order for the profitability to be assessed – independently of the lawyer seeking to introduce the business – from the firm's perspective. Further, this assessment needs to be viewed not as a roadblock to client development, but as a pathway to improving the firm's bottom line. If management is willing to recognize the value of making better front-end evaluation of client suitability as a threshold matter of policy, it can then decide to assign the task either to general counsel, or to involve the firm's financial staff in establishing parameters for client financial suitability. Some firms choose a third path, creating a separate new business intake department, with input from both general counsel and the financial staff – but where the ultimate decision whether or not to accept business is shared by the general counsel and the firm's senior leadership.

Creating effective financial intake parameters requires serious effort. Initially, firms' CFOs, billing departments, and controllers need to mine their existing client data to determine the common characteristics of clients that do not pay the firm's bills. The analysis should have as its goal to identify patterns. Are problems coming from certain identifiable groups or categories of clients? For example, does a firm have a much greater problem collecting from individual, as opposed to corporate, clients? Or from certain kinds of businesses, or types of transaction or litigation? Do certain lines of business incur significant overhead costs but routinely yield no profits, or worse yet, losses?

Once the categories of unprofitable clients and matters are identified, firms can create parameters for use during intake evaluation which identify prospective matters as requiring special review and approval. For example, in what circumstance should the firm consider setting a minimum advance deposit retainer for prospective clients, and what thresholds should apply to different categories and different types of matters? Then, if prospective clients are unwilling or unable to meet the established parameters, this should be a red flag for the client's willingness or ability to pay as the matter proceed, and, absent some compelling reason, should lead to the rejection of the work.

In the post-recession world, even though tensions can be created within firms by the adoption of these sound business protocols, good risk management suggests that it is critical for firms to identify which clients are likely to be profitable, and which are likely to create problems, and to make intake decisions based upon that analysis.

A tightening legal market results in great temptation on the part of lawyers to "dabble", in other words to take on work outside their field of expertise, resulting in legal errors that lead to claims. Dabbling is also something a good intake system can manage if it is structured so as to identify who is doing what work, and permit the evaluation of whether this lawyer is the appropriate one to be handling this kind of work before the matter is accepted.

Once firms have decided to adopt this approach to client intake evaluation, the next question is what can be done to simplify, and automate, the decision-making process. Software can sort matters into the suitability parameters established by the firm. The appropriate parameters for this kind of automatic screening include the following: no outstanding accounts receivable from the client; that the work to be done is the kind that the firm has the skills to perform, and is actually going to be handled by a lawyer within the appropriate practice group; and that the revenue to be generated will exceed the cost of providing the services.

On the other end of the scale, if the prospective client has no established positive history with the firm, is seeking assistance in a practice area where the firm has a negative collection experience, or is unwilling or unable to pay a retainer that the firm's financial group has identified as the minimum that is appropriate for the matter, that matter should be rejected automatically, absent specific re-evaluation by and approval of firm management.

When an intake request doesn't get a "clean" pass or fail on financial suitability after this automatic evaluation process, the request should be escalated, and reviewed by a business intake manager (or, less efficiently but common in some firms) by a committee designated to make these decisions, but in any event not by the partner seeking to introduce the business. Ultimately, client intake management should become a systematized, objective, and uniform process in which decision-making is independent, thereby improving management of the firm's risks.

Because this type of structure often involves significant changes from prior practice, risk managers need to get buy-in from the firm's lawyers and the firm's management. Lawyers are likely to comply – and may even welcome the new arrangements – if it can be shown that the time they are required to dedicate to the intake process is simplified, and that they will no longer be faced with voluminous conflict reports that are hard to read, and even harder to understand. The more the firm can demonstrate that the new arrangements will operate quickly and efficiently, consistent with the objectives of taking on good clients and weeding out bad clients, the more likely lawyers will support the system. In turn, this buy-in will allow management to take the necessary steps to ensure compliance throughout the firm, based on the common objective that better client intake management will improve profitability.

Making the intake process work efficiently and promptly

The intake system must work speedily and efficiently. But in order to succeed it must receive all of the information needed on which to base decisions. If prospective new client matters are not made and communicated on an expeditious basis, lawyers feel compelled to start work, in order to avoid client prejudice (and not to lose the business). And if it later turns out that the firm decides that the matter should not have been taken it on in the first place, the firm is left with a big write-off, and a serious ethical problem in connection with withdrawal. Beyond these problems, the time it takes for the firm to sort this all out, is non-billable and entirely unproductive.

Engagement letters/fee agreements

Every attorney client relationship should begin with an engagement letter. This should clearly address all of the parameters of the attorney client relationship, and should be hard wired into the intake system as a prerequisite for opening any new client engagement.

Not only will this establish uniformity, it will also simplify the process for file opening, again reducing the time needed for compliance. In addition to any terms required by ethical rules, other terms engagement letters should address are:

- accurate client identification and contact information;
- a carefully defined scope of the representation;
- identification of how and with whom the law firm will be communicating;
- circumstances for withdrawal;
- fees, costs, retainers; and
- file retention.

In addition, if the firm wishes to have an arbitration clause to aid dispute resolution (after checking with its insurance carrier), arbitration terms should be included as well.

Because the forms will be standardized and mandatory for all clients, variances from the standard form that may be needed in individual matters can be quickly identified and sent for approval to the firm's general counsel or financial manager, as appropriate.

Firms need to use the intake system to enforce the use of the approved forms. Client and matter billing numbers should not be issued, and there should be no ability to record or enter time on any matter unless and until the firm receives a countersigned engagement letter. A less onerous alternative is to assign a file number once an engagement letter has been sent to the client, but then the firm needs to monitor the matter and close it down if a countersigned engagement letter is not received within "x" days.

The requirement of an engagement letter countersigned by the client is a critical milestone in the relationship. Without a countersigned engagement letter, a law firm may find itself in the world of quantum meruit recovery for its services. More importantly, from a purely practical perspective, a good attorney client relationship is based on trust and confidence that runs both ways. If a client will not sign an engagement letter, firms must ask themselves what else will the client not sign? And if a client is unwilling to accede to the request for a countersigned engagement letter from the very beginning, what type of cooperation can the firm expect from that client in the matter itself?

Conclusion

Effective client intake takes effort and discipline both on the part of firms and individual lawyers. But once the system is up and working, a law firm can use the client intake process to create a path to improved profitability as well as saving itself serious and costly problems later.

Chapter 10:
X-raying matters – how to improve matter risk management

By Peter Bennett, COO, Bates Wells Braithwaite (London) LLP

Key takeaway points

1. Focused matter-level risk management can reduce your PII premiums.
2. Identify your firm's 20 percent of high risk and concentrate on managing it.
3. Ensure your partners know that their highest-risk matters will be scrutinized.
4. Leverage existing technology to improve operational risk management.
5. Make risk management part of the fee-earning process; it is essential to adoption.
6. Explain why risk management is important; don't assume everyone understands. Education is key to ongoing adherence.
7. Do not be afraid to publicize how well you manage your risks – clients will want to know.
8. There are only two universal risks – read to the end of the chapter for the secrets of reducing your PII Premium.

In 2006, I conceived and installed a simple, but devastatingly effective, matter-level risk management system, which is now used by every fee earner at our firm, on every new matter.

It takes two to three minutes for the fee earner to use and has gained the highest level of immediate fee-earner compliance. It is now undertaken 100 percent of the time – without grumbles from the fee earners and partners.

The impact of the system was immediate, long-lasting and dramatic in reducing the number of reported professional liability incidents and, more importantly, professional indemnity (PII) claims. That, more quickly than we had hoped, led to a dramatic reduction in our PII premium annual costs. We have saved Bates Wells & Braithwaite £6 million since 2006, and over £900,000 on the 2015 renewal. Approaching our 2016 PII renewal we are aiming for a further major premium reduction based upon nine years of no pay-outs by our commercial underwriters.

Figure 1 shows what we would have paid had we kept our 2006 premium rating and compares that with our actual payments. Figure 2 shows our annual savings over the 2006 PII rates. Figure 3 shows our PII insurance pay-outs total after the risk management system was introduced in 2006 and Figure 4 shows the impact it had on PII claims needing cash reserves/pay-outs.

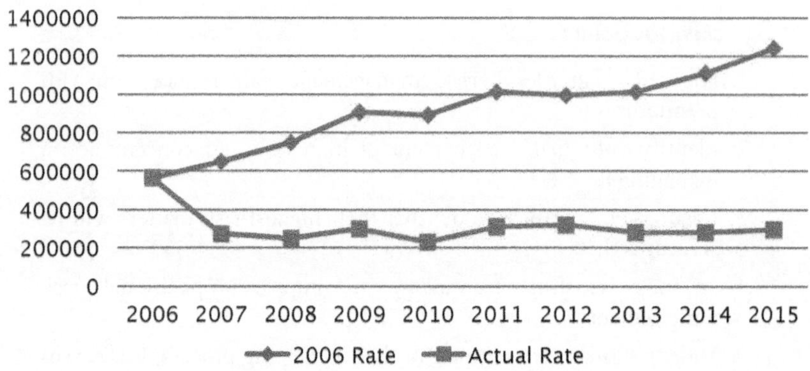

Figure 1: BWB PII premium 2006–15

Figure 2 shows our annual savings over the 2006 PII rates.

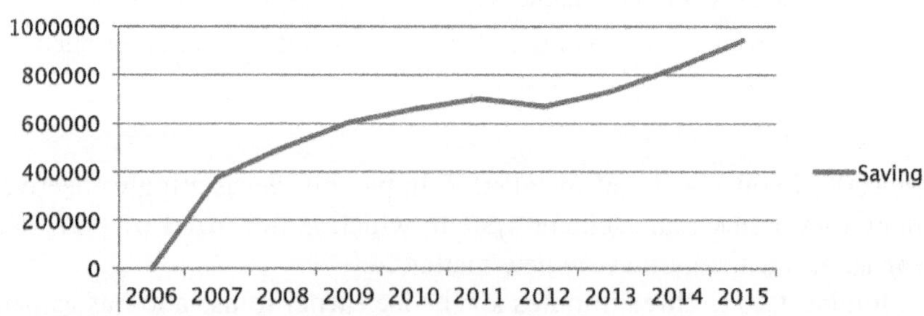

Figure 2: BWB PII premium saving per year over 2006 rates

Figure 3 shows our PII insurance pay-outs total after the risk management system was introduced in 2006.

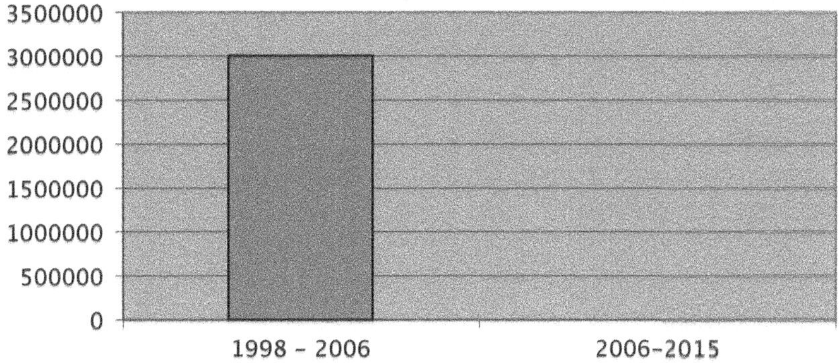

Figure 3: PII insurance payouts £ total

Figure 4 shows the impact it had on PII claims needing cash reserves/pay-outs.

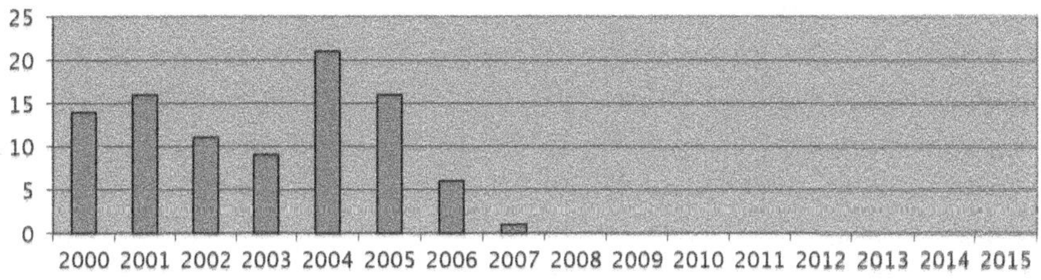

Figure 4: PII claims needing £ reserves/payouts

I hope the demonstrated benefits of the matter-level risk management system make it worth you reading the rest of this chapter, because it has universal application and has developed into a bottom-up management information system of unique power.

The eureka moment

The risk management system was conceived in a 'eureka' moment in 2006. Our PII premiums were very high and getting higher, with a spate of recent large claims.

The first PII renewal after my arrival as COO was difficult and expensive. That spurred me to read the solicitors' reports prepared for the PII underwriters on every claim the firm had suffered for 15 years. The reports are detailed – about 10 pages each – and are factual and unbiased. I suspect I was the only chief officer in any law firm who had ever read these reports in such detail.

As I read each one, a pattern began to clearly emerge of common risk factors. After reading all 15 years' worth of reports, I realized that the risk factors established in my mind after reading the first 50 percent had not changed after I had finished reading them all.

As COO, I was able to realize my ideas by working with our talented head of IT to produce a risk management system based on that stable and universal group of risk factors.

Creating the system

The firm's IT manager and I analyzed the best way to create such a solution. Very quickly, it emerged that the fastest and most cost-effective way of developing such a system was to leverage our existing technology. We created a risk management solution within our legal workflow and case management system, Lexis Visualfiles.

The benefits of this approach were many. Foremost, the in-built developmental capabilities offered by the technology meant that the risk management solution was easy and quick to develop. Because we were expanding the functionality of an existing, already-deployed technology, we did not incur any additional software costs or even have to purchase additional user licenses.

Furthermore, the system was well understood by the IT team, so no new skills were required to create the solution. Familiarity goes a long way in user adoption – with the fee earners already using the system on a day-to-day basis, securing their buy-in to the new risk management solution was not an issue, as often tends to be the case with new technology. We embedded the risk management system into the existing fee-earner productivity tools in the client management system (CMS). In essence, creating the solution within our existing system delivered the return on investment.

How it works

The core risk management system works, as follows.

Every new matter has a risk assessment undertaken by the matter fee earner. This is a simple one-page screen with multiple-choice answers that takes two to three minutes to complete. An instant risk classification then comes on screen and is printed. If the score is 'danger' or 'very high' risk, the paper result has to go to the supervising partner for review and a signature of approval.

The frequency of danger-level risk assessments is relatively rare in most departments. Because of this, partners are prepared to give the risk assessment results proper attention.

The risk score sheet covers three points:

1. The risk assessment bands 'low' to 'danger' together with a score sheet showing the weightings that have led to the risk assessment – what is the unique combination of risk factors that are driving a high-risk score? Those scores point the partner to ways of managing those risk factors.
2. Users are given information on the money-laundering risk band and score – again rated between 'low' and 'danger', with the scores pointing to the anti-money-laundering (AML) management strategy for danger-level matters.
3. The risk score is compared with the estimate that has been placed on the matter. Where we have a danger matter and a low estimate, a message is given to the partner that the estimate should be renegotiated (almost, but not quite 'you must be joking with that estimate and this risk!'). If it is not possible to renegotiate the fee then, as a minimum, the signed terms and conditions must limit liability to £3 million.

Partners have to sign that they have understood the risks involved and are confident that the risks can be managed. Lawyers do not like signing an assurance that they know to be incorrect. It is the educative process of partners regularly and routinely examining the risk factors and deciding on the appropriate action to be taken that has revolutionized the risk environment at our firm.

Partner risk-management actions

On a broader front, having the wrong team working on a matter will probably mean it will:

- Take longer;
- Exceed the estimate;
- Be less profitable; and
- Result in arguments over the bill, grumbles, formal complaints and, in the extreme, a negligence claim.

The following simple risk management actions are used by partners to manage matter risks.

1. If the matter is more complex and of higher value than the partner had realized when they had casually passed it to a junior fee earner, this can be dealt with simply by passing it to a more senior fee earner, who repeats the risk assessment.
2. If the matter may be more specialized than the partner had envisaged and the partner did not realize that the allocated fee-earner had no expertise in the specialist field, simply reallocating the matter to a fee earner with the required expertise will reduce the risk.
3. If the answer to the risk question 'is there a single point of catastrophic failure?' is yes, the partner is encouraged to determine what those points of failure are and to manage them accordingly. Often, the single point of catastrophic failure relates to the central purpose of the transaction. On the same set of legal circumstances, the single point of catastrophic failure can be different or non-existent, depending upon the intentions of the client.
4. There will come a point when the partner has examined the risk factors and come to the conclusion that this is a large and complex matter, capable of catastrophic failure, no one in the firm has relevant expertise and there are no credible ways of managing that potential failure. The only and obvious conclusion is that the firm should refuse to undertake what could be an incredibly dangerous transaction (but with a temptingly large fee!).

Second-tier management

At the same time as the risk assessment results come off the printer for review by the partner, 'danger' and 'high risk' matters are sent (with identical information) by email to the risk manager, the AML officer and the reputational risk group – but targeted e-mails driven by the risks identified within the matter. As explained below, each second-tier manager only receives notification of high-risk matters as scored and weighted on their own risk criteria.

1. Risk manager

The 'danger' email to the risk manager will often lead to a simple call to the partner to ask about that matter and what action is being taken to manage the risks. The discussions between the risk managers and the partners reinforce in the partners' minds the need to take risks seriously. It is sometimes the risk manager who will force the decision that we should not take on a danger-level matter that cannot be risk-managed safely.

2. Anti-money laundering officer

Having a matter-level risk-based instant alert to the AML officer provides great comfort in terms of compliance. The AML officer can concentrate personally on the real money-laundering 'danger' matters and clients.

We have a maximum period for the review of the AML check on each client, depending upon the risk profile of the legal entity. The number of danger or high-risk level matters that are recorded against a particular client automatically brings forward the date for its AML review.

If there are a number of danger-level matters within a short period, this will bring forward an immediate AML review of the client, not just the transaction.

3. Reputational risk

The first addition to the risk questions was a new simple reputational risk question for partners. We have a high reputation to protect as a 'City firm with a conscience'. If a fee earner flags any reputational risk in a matter, it is filtered for a review and then forwarded to the Reputational Risks and Conflicts group if concerns are valid.

Risk maps

All of the results of the risk assessments can be viewed within a database environment, with color coding of 'high risk' (orange) and 'danger' matters (red).

These produce a risk map that identifies clusters of high-risk and danger-level matters around particular fee earners, partners or departments. The database can also show risk clusters around particular clients or introducers.

It was almost shocking when we first viewed our risk map and saw that the risk clusters were exactly mapping the areas of our previous PII claims.

The strength of the risk map is that resources can be concentrated on those areas that are regularly managing high risk (but probably very well paid) matters. It also means that the regulatory activity can be lightened on departments that consistently deal with low-risk matters. The same mapping technique is used to identify clusters of money laundering risk and reputational risk.

Risk-based file reviews

In the past, we had asked for randomly selected files to be reviewed at regular intervals. Partners then generally selected the thinnest files they could find.

We now centrally select the highest risk matters for each fee earner. For fee earners or partners with danger-level matters, all of these danger matters are subject to file review.

The fact that partners know that their highest risk matters will be subject to file review means that they maintain vigilance in managing those matters.

The second eureka moment

I later had a second eureka moment – a realization that the matter level risk assessment was in effect creating a unique 'barcode' for every matter our partners and fee earners handled. After 10 years we now have 40,000 uniquely barcoded matters.

The simple risk screen – originally 10, now 20, multiple-choice questions – isolates the 20 percent of those matters that need real management focus. Just as importantly, it identifies the 80 percent of matters that are routine and low risk, and which can be dealt with by a light regulatory and management regime – the Pareto Principle in action.

However, the system is more intelligent than this implies. Each question has a simple multiple-choice answer – yes or no, core area or outer fringe, level one to level five. Those answers are translated into numeric scores.

Individual scores are permanently attached to a matter and become the equivalent of a product barcode. Once there, it can be read and differently weighted for an infinite number of management, risk and reporting purposes.

By way of example, we have a matter whose answers to the 20 risk questions results in a 'danger' rating for PII risk, medium-level money laundering risk and nil reputational risk. This automatically triggers the following 10 actions:

1. The partner must consider the risk, take action to manage that risk and then sign to say he considered the risk factors and that he can manage the risk.
2. The partner is asked to review the estimate if it is too low for the risk score.
3. If the estimate is not done yet, it will automatically be given a 15 percent increase for the danger risk factor, with our estimator tool.
4. The matter will be closed down if we do not have signed terms and conditions within a stipulated number of days.

5. The risk manager will be alerted by email and will call the partner.
6. The matter (along with the fee earner/partner etc.) will appear red on the risk map.
7. If the fee earner answers 'manic' to the question on his level of busyness, he will be named within the busyness barometer, which will rise by that answer.
8. The matter will be subject to file review every six months.
9. The medium money-laundering risk will increase the PII risk score by a minor amount. The AML officer will not be alerted, but it will bring forward the client's AML review date by a few weeks.
10. As the matter is assessed as having no reputational risk, this will simply be reported on the partner's score sheet.

All of those actions (and many more when I think of them over time) are all based on the barcode. That barcode is linked to the matter and client codes, the fee earner, partner, client partner, introducer, department and country codes and any other code on your systems that link to any of these.

Each PII risk, money laundering risk and reputational risk weighs (or ignores) each number of the bar code in a different way, to create its own risk result.

If your firm has a presence in England and/or Wales, your list of 'danger' matters should be the main content of your firm's risk register, which is required by the Solicitors Regulation Authority.

Impact on the firm

PII notifications and claims fell to virtually nil as soon as we introduced this system in 2006. As each year of no claims went by and the cost of PII premiums fell and then plummeted, the evidence that it was due to this risk management system became stronger, then overwhelming.

Since implementing our risk management system, we have been able to concentrate all of our efforts on identifying and managing the 20 percent of genuinely high-risk matters – high risk for claims, for money laundering and for reputational risk. Taken together, the system forces risk management into the day-to-day culture of partners, risk managers and the management board.

The system has self-re-enforcing waves, starting with the pause for thought before a partner signs that he can manage a high-risk matter, re-enforced by notification and action by the risk manager, AML officer and/or reputation manager, followed by the risk maps which provide a board-level strategic understanding of risk clusters and the independent risk-based file reviews. Each of these puts pressure on everyone to conduct and manage dangerous matters to the highest standards – and picks up on those partners who do not manage risks well.

Improving risk management

We have come a long way since we first adopted risk management strategically. Risk management is now a default discipline at BWB. In fact, it has transformed our culture – unlike previously and in most traditional law firms, individual partners no longer have the authority to override firm policies. More importantly, partners do not want to supersede policies anymore – the system provides evidence and irrefutable information based on business rationale analysis.

When we first instituted the system, the information given to partners to assist with managing risk was generic. For example, the danger-level score may have been triggered because the matter was complex or of high value. However, today, the information provided to partners on high-risk matters articulates the specific factors that are driving the risk, along with suggested actions required to manage the specific risks within the matter. This is enabled by the algorithms in the risk-management solution.

For example, a question asks if there is a single point of catastrophic failure. If the answer is affirmative, the partner is advised to understand exactly where the single point of catastrophic failure resides and what steps are required to manage, such as requesting a second partner to review key documents or instructing counsel to appraise clauses.

In some vital areas such as personal conflicts and working outside of the firm's areas of expertise, the risk management system applies a two-level check to enforce policy. In select high-danger situations, a matter can even be closed down unless two partners have evaluated and approved for it to continue. Then again, a matter may still be closed down, unless fee earners working on the task along with the partners in question are able to persuade the management board/risk manager/anti-money laundering (AML) reporting officer that it is safe for the matter to remain open.

We first developed this matter closedown process for credit control, followed by credit exposure and compliance. It has now been adapted for risk. It serves as a very powerful and unwavering tool to execute policy and compliance in the firm.

Expanding the scope

In the past 18 months, we have further expanded the scope of the matter level risk assessment to cover personal sensitive data, market sensitive data, newsworthy data, conflict, own interest conflict, fees over £100,000, and PII liability over £10 million and over our PII limit. All of these are extremely complex areas of risk that are traditionally hard to manage. Once identified as a high risk in each category a complex set of targeted actions are automatically generated.

Take reputational risk: we proactively prevent any potential brand damage that may come from taking on new clients or matters. The risk management system does not take the decision, but it does isolate the 2–3 percent of matters/clients which must be reviewed by our reputational risk group before fee earners are allowed to proceed. Undertaking an in-depth matter risk assessment pre-empts failure and protects the firm's reputation.

Today, data loss presents an extremely high risk to law firms – and not just from the Information Commissioner's Office (ICO) by way of large penalties. Breaches of highly confidential client information can result in devastating repercussions for the firm and its clients.

For every matter, the fee earner has to offer a view on the seriousness of any potential data breach in three areas on a scale of one to five. 'One' refers to serious but standard damage which any client data loss would involve, while 'five' signifies something that would be deeply damaging. Those three areas/questions are personal sensitive data, market sensitive data and newsworthy data.

This kind of risk indication guides partners in devising measures to ensure the most sensitive client data is protected as securely as possible. In fact, this approach has made data security a board-level agenda item in our firm. In this area, a danger matter requires partners to confirm that they are adhering to our '20 point data security protocol' for the danger matter.

When the three data questions were first introduced we had several departments complaining that vast numbers of their cases would be 'danger' and require special measures, and asking for the risk questions to be 'watered down'. That proved to be a fantastic educational opportunity. Eventually they accepted their matters were dangerous, that a loss would probably mean a report to the ICO, which virtually automatically means a material breach report to the SRA… and once that acceptance was in place who could argue that the sensible measures in our 20-point data security plan were unreasonable?

Similarly, the introduction of a simple new question: 'Will you be managing a conflict?' brought a deluge of new conflicts to the center for review on a scale that was previously hidden. Some of those conflicts were being well managed by experienced partners who understood the complexities of the SRA conflict rules, but many were not.

A related question 'as far as you are aware is anyone at BWB personally involved in this matter' bought a number of important own interest conflicts to the surface. It is amazing how a lawyer would never dream of straying outside of their area of expertise... until the corporate lawyer suddenly becomes a litigator or a probate lawyer for a member of their family!

Client risk assessment

We have now grown to a size (£25 million/250 staff) when we can centralize our client on-boarding process and are currently piloting on spreadsheets a similar approach to client risk assessment. We have established 35 client risk criteria each with a drop-down menu of replies. However only 10 of those need to be dealt with by the partner, and even then, most are 'as far as you are aware' questions that can be answered quickly. The rest are dealt with by the central client on-boarding administrator who has knowledge after completing the AML and client conflict checks. Again, the principle is to identify the small number of higher risk clients and send them up the management chain for review and decisions – ultimately by our reputational risk and conflicts group.

Once that system has been piloted in this form, it will be placed within a Visual Files developed risk screen similar to matter level risk and a risk score attached to the client – when the risk is being managed rather than the potential client rejected. Then the higher client level risk score will be combined with matter level risk result so that an identical matter which would be accepted from a 'safe' client would be subject to much higher scrutiny and test from a higher risk client.

What are the 35 client level risk indicators? They vary from the base country of the client to the countries where they operate, credit ratings, deliberately opaque ownership, a range of industries considered socially irresponsible and many more – while some of these will be the same for all firms, some relate to reputational risk – which BWB regards as the highest risk which requires the greatest scrutiny to defend our hard-won reputation.

Future plans

We feel there is still scope to improve our risk management system further. We are creating special screens within the system solely for the central risk team, to give them comprehensive visibility of all the danger-level risks of the firm.

Originally, the risk management system was designed to highlight the top 5 percent of danger-level matters for the immediate attention the appropriate senior managers and ultimately the management board. With the risk management system having been fine-tuned over the years, we are seeing much higher numbers of danger-level matters.

Today, we have developed a good understanding of how real the danger-level risks are and how effectively the partners are able to mitigate them. This additional mechanism within the system allows the central risk management team to further investigate the high-risk matters to provide a more realistic assessment of the likelihood of the risk happening. This final filter will help to take some matters originally judged as high risk off the danger-level list. Often, many danger-level matters are highly profitable, so a more in-depth evaluation of their risk level is essential.

Given the debilitating impact of a money laundering accusation, AML risk management is a major priority for our firm. We are implementing measures that take the management of this element further. We are integrating the AML risk generated from the risk management system with data completed by the AML investigators via a specialist AML reporting service.

Our AML reports are very good, but require human review to answer results queries such as:

- Is this PEP our PEP?;
- Does that group structure require further reports?
- Can we explain that low credit score?
- How much weight should we give to the three special-interest persons? and
- The risk management system flagged an overseas client, but the AML report amplifies the risk by showing the legal entity is based in Iran rather than a low-risk overseas territory such as Ireland.

We are placing those results within the same simple question-and-answer screens and weighting answers as per the risk management system to increase or decrease the AML risk profile for clients. Sometimes, this process pushes the risk level into a 'no' but, at other times, it allows us to create a special AML status on the client of 'AML high risk', i.e., caution is needed, enabling us to monitor and apply special conditions to any matters that are opened for those clients. This converts the AML process from a simple good defense at the time of entry into a long-term risk management tool.

Over the past three years, BWB has faced two major risk-related challenges. Our management board has instinctively looked to our risk management system as the go-to tool to help deal with them. In both cases, we have successfully used the risk management system to demonstrate to regulators the measures that we have taken to prevent their reoccurrence. Today, 60 percent of our monthly 10 page COLP/COFA reports are derived from our risk management system.

The ability to screen out the small number of danger-level matters for management review has produced an amazing number of very interesting, diverse, profitable but risky matters which were previously below the radar. Routinely receiving information about these matters that are a potential danger for PII claims, AML, reputation, data sensitivity and conflicts gives me, the partners and the management board the necessary information to actively manage our 4,000 new matters each year. Our risk management system ensures that we are successfully managing our surprisingly diverse, interesting, profitable, but potentially high-risk caseload.

The core secrets of PII risks – or how to reduce your PII claims and premiums

After 10 years, 40,000 matter level risk assessments, around 1,000 danger matters being managed successfully, without our PII underwriters paying out once – what are the universal risks which we have identified and successfully managed? There are only two, which apply to every law firm and every professional services firm in every jurisdiction in the world.

It is not the value of the transaction. Experienced teams who undertake the same large transaction for £10 million each time are a low risk – it is their core expertise and they are very good at handling that transaction. We ask for the size of the potential liability as only when combined with the real risk factors, it alerts you to the size of the potential claim and that is very important.

Core risk no 1 – Does this transaction have a single point of catastrophic failure?

In many transactions – even ones involving multi-million transactions – however bad a mistake the lawyer makes they cannot destroy the underlying value. Conversely, in other matters a single error can destroy value. Forcing the partner to understand that there is a single point of catastrophic failure, pinpointing it exactly and requiring that to be appropriately managed (or we refuse the transaction) is key to reducing your PII claims and premiums.

Core risk no 2 – Is this lawyer competent to undertake this matter?

Most lawyers understand this most of the time but pressure of work, lucrative fees, needing to hit budget, doing it for granny, an assistant not wanting to own up to lack of experience, can all lead to danger. We have a number of risk questions that really probe on competence. A question offers a list to describe competence to undertake this matter with the answers being from 'core expertise' to 'no expertise'. A second asks how many similar matters have you dealt with in the last year? A third is 'is this service on our website?' A fourth asks if there is any personal involvement by anyone in the firm with this matter. A fifth asks if the total fees are over £100,000 and combines that with the number of similar transactions in the last year. A team who have competence at transactions generating a fee of £10,000 are in danger when they try to take on one with fees of £200,000 and when they answer 'no similar transactions in the last year', we have to upgrade the team or refuse the work.

That is it – the secret to reduce your PII claims and PII premium costs.

To summarize what you have to do in a single sentence: *Identify the small number of matters where lawyers who are not competent to undertake a transaction ('straying from their competence' is a kinder description), who are proposing to take on a matter that has a single point of catastrophic failure and if they trigger that failure, the result will be a high-value PII claim against your firm.*

Our risk maps and our previous claims record showed clearly that claims are not 'bad luck' or 'bad lawyers'. Some lawyers have a regular stream of potentially high-risk matters. If those high-risk matters are not identified and managed properly, an error will inevitably be made and a PII claim received, and your PII premiums will inevitably increase.

For readers only interested in reducing their PII premiums the above sentence in italics is what you will take out of this chapter. For readers interested in law firm management generally, the concept and power of a barcode on every single matter in the firm, is as potentially revolutionary in the management of law as it has been in the management of supermarkets – think about it.

A version of this case study first appeared in Managing Partner *magazine in February 2013. Fully revised and updated in 2016.*